PRAISE FOR *TOCQUEVILLE IN ARABIA*

"*Tocqueville in Arabia* is a searching and eloquent meditation concerning the impact of the democratic spirit on students in a turbulent Middle East where the idea of equality has arrived recently and has been refracted through distinctive cultural, political, and religious lenses as well as on students in America, where the idea of equality has advanced far and wide. Joshua Mitchell weaves together keen observations of his students in Qatar and Iraq and at Georgetown University in Washington, subtle reflections on his lifetime of ties to the Arab word, and deft exposition of works of political philosophy, especially Tocqueville but with astute attention also given to Rousseau, Smith, and Marx. By throwing into sharp relief the expectations, aspirations, and anxieties that characterize young men and women today in regions of the world unequally touched by the spirit of equality, Mitchell illuminates the future of democracy and freedom."

—Peter Berkowitz, Hoover Institution, Stanford University

"Tocqueville taught us how much can be learned about one culture seen through the lens of someone intelligent and sympathetic from another. Joshua Mitchell knows Tocqueville and Arabia, and his readers will come to know both better."

—George F. Will

"In *Tocqueville in Arabia,* Joshua Mitchell explores the Middle East as a gifted scholar and a brilliant teacher. His book is an enticing and courageous reading of contemporary life among the younger generation in the Middle East, and a sober account of the challenges to modernity that lay ahead. This remarkable book, which draws on the philosophical writings of Tocqueville without being arcane or tendentious, illuminates what is going on in the hearts and minds of young people in the Middle East—and in America too. *Tocqueville in Arabia* is

T0004196

an outstanding example of how scholarship can shed light on the march of democracy and equality in our times."
—Yossi Shain, Georgetown University

"*Tocqueville in Arabia* succeeds in a task that would have seemed nearly impossible—that of making Tocqueville, who is often pressed into service to comment on contemporary American life, a plausible commentator on the contemporary Middle East.... [Mitchell] argues that support for liberal arts education in the Middle East is essential. His view may seem quixotic, but he makes a powerful case that it is the long view—and the right one."
—*American Conservative*

"Like Alexis de Tocqueville and his classic account *Democracy in America*, Joshua Mitchell analyzes the potential for democracy in the Middle East post–Arab Spring, offering clarity on the troubled present and an optimistic view of the future."
—*Barnes & Noble Review*

"Joshua Mitchell's *Tocqueville in Arabia* is a many-sided book. Part memoir, part geopolitical analysis, part rumination on the souls of the young—focus your reading one way and Mitchell proposes an understanding of the Middle East based on the spiritual sociology of Alexis de Tocqueville. Focus your reading another way and he offers a teacher's commentary on the tastes and mental habits of elite university students in Qatar, Iraq, and the United States. Taken together, this short book honors and inhabits Tocqueville's method and voice, illuminating the essence of liberal modernity by the lights of the Middle East and the inner consciousness of the Arab world by the prospect of a dawning modernity.... Mitchell's experiences in the Middle East and his ruminations about higher education breathe new life into Tocqueville's thought just as Tocqueville elucidates the Arab world's encounter with democratic modernity. Creative, learned, at its best *Tocqueville in Arabia* is a model for political theory to analyze one of the titanic political struggles of our age."

—*National Interest*

"A personal and passionate meditation.... Mitchell provides an excellent demonstration of the ways in which Tocqueville's modes of analysis and insights can be updated to shed more light on major issues confronting democratic societies like our own and those in the making. It also offers the basis for a genuine conversation between conservative and liberal readings of Tocqueville concerning the future of democracy in the twenty-first century and the validity of alternative paths to the preservation of freedom."

—*Perspectives on Politics*

"Mitchell brings his long experience of the Middle East to bear in *Tocqueville in Arabia*. The result is an intriguing, insightful, sometimes profound study of the effects of the democratic age on the human condition."

—*Society*

"Mitchell's style of personal storytelling engages the reader and his original application of Tocqueville's 'democratic man' to a Middle Eastern context proves to be valuable, especially in the wake of the Arab Spring."

—*Political Studies Review*

TOCQUEVILLE IN ARABIA

TOCQUEVILLE
in ARABIA

The Anxieties of the Democratic Age

JOSHUA MITCHELL

New York • London

First paperback edition published in 2023 by Encounter
Books, an activity of Encounter for Culture and Education,
Inc., a nonprofit, tax-exempt corporation.
Encounter Books website address:
www.encounterbooks.com

Manufactured in the United States and printed on
acid-free paper. The paper used in this publication meets
the minimum requirements of ANSI/NISO Z39.48-1992
(R 1997) (*Permanence of Paper*).

FIRST PAPERBACK EDITION

First hardcover edition published in 2013 by The University
of Chicago Press
Hardcover edition ISBN: 978-0-22608-731-3

Library of Congress Cataloging-in-Publication Data is
available under
ISBN 978-1-64177-313-3 (paperback)
ISBN 978-1-64177-314-0 (ebook)

1 2 3 4 5 6 7 8 9 20 23

I undertook to see, not differently, but further than the parties;
and while they are occupied with the next day,
I have wanted to ponder the future.

ALEXIS DE TOCQUEVILLE, *Democracy in America*

CONTENTS

Preface to the Paperback Edition

Originally published by University of Chicago Press in 2013 under the title *Tocqueville in Arabia: Dilemmas in a Democratic Age*, the book before you, excepting this preface to the first paperback edition, appeared at a time of growing Middle East fatigue in America. The American mood, giddy and triumphal after the 1991 Gulf War, darkened into intermixed rage and despair after the ghastly live-broadcast death-spectacle in New York and in Washington that sun-lit morning of September 11, 2001. What followed in the way of primitive, not to say unjustified, retribution in the distant mountains and high plateaus of Afghanistan soon transformed and metastasized. Thin is the line between commensurate response and pride. On April 9, 2003, less than nineteen months later, Baghdad fell to American forces who were now at war with two nations, markedly different from one another, each an inscrutable mystery to our military, to our intelligence agencies, and to all but a few remaining academics who had been trained before gaming and simulations came to constitute due diligence. They do not.

Tocqueville is well-known for having invented the idea of American exceptionalism. There, in the Author's Introduction to his 1835 masterpiece, *Democracy in America*, he announced that the term does not mean America is *special*. It means that America is the exception to the rule. What is the rule? The rule is that all the world now has, or once had, aristocratic social conditions. Not least, the Middle East, I add. America is the exception. America was born into democratic social conditions, more or less. This difference has momentous implications we must understand if we wish our nation to act wisely in the world. The vast swath of the world that retains its aristocratic social conditions, or is in some transitional phase away from them, will see in America *both* a rosy promise of liberation from the burden of its own aristocratic past and the haunting prospect of a disorderly, lonely, decadent, Godless future. America for citizens of these nations is not America; she is a Rorschach image welling up from the primordial aristocratic psychic depth, about which Americans, without long training, have little understanding. This means that many, indeed most, of the nations around the world will respond to America by oscillating between reverence and repulsion. As Americans, we should not be surprised when we encounter these fraternal twins. As Americans, too, we must be mindful that our initial judgments about the rest of the world are probably wrong, not because we lack intelligence, but because we lack understanding of a type of humanity—aristocratic man, as Tocqueville called him—that precedes us, and still dwells among us. I do not doubt that the burden of empire still falls on American shoulders. Since the end of World War II, it has largely rested on us to keep the sea lanes open, to be the de facto enforcer of international law. I do doubt that we can perform that task well without understanding that the rest of the world is not like us. We talk endlessly in America today about diversity and inclusion, but harbor an egalitarian prejudice about what these terms must mean. When citizens from other nations hear us declare on the international stage that we respect, encourage, *and demand* diversity and inclusion on a global scale, and then discover that precisely what they themselves believe—about shame, honor, decorum, remembrance, ritual, men, women, family, government, religion, etc.—is shameful and dishonorable and has no place in the civilized world, they do not conclude that American self-understanding is capacious, but rather that it is impaired by a prejudice it does not grasp that it imposes, that its purportedly universal values are parochial rather than universal. "Man's idea of unity," Tocqueville wrote, "is always small and sterile; only God's is grand and fertile." This must especially be true when a nation with a democratic soul is surrounded by a vast sea of aristocratic-souled nations, and does not even recognize it. Chapter 1, "Colliding and Converging Worlds," offers an account, more personal than historical, of the long journey—from the Yemen and Kuwait of my youth, to teaching for Georgetown in Washington, to brief stints in Buenos Aires and Lisbon, and finally to my time in Doha—that brought me to understand the peculiar standing of democratic America in a world that is, for all intents and purposes, very aristocratic.

How should Americans proceed with this knowledge that the rest of the world is aristocratic, unlike us? The whole of *Tocqueville in Arabia* was intended to begin to answer that question. I say *begin* to answer it, because the new subtitle, *The Anxieties of the Democratic Age*, indicates more emphatically than I let on a decade ago that there can be no unequivocal, formulaic answer. Recognizing that this new, democratic age that lay ahead was one without principled answers to the questions it posed, Tocqueville wrote, "the entirety of *Democracy in America* has been written with a kind of religious dread." As the aristocratic age came to an end, the venerated wisdom of the fathers would be abandoned, along with long-inherited social relations that anchored such wisdom in lived practices; in its place, novelty would succeed novelty, and the democratic mind and heart would find no stable place of rest. It would be free—but free as a truant is free, without constraint, wandering through the world, homeless, Godless, and alone. For that dis-ease, an antidote would be needed, which would be difficult to accept, and more difficult still to administer, because no one would have the authority to administer it. Democratic man would *need* to be gathered together with others; yet centripetal inclinations within, and social breakdown without, would drive him into his own thoughts and sentiments, there to judge the world alone. Every social ar-

rangement would seem artificial, held fast with the illegiti-
mate adhesive of power, and therefore in need of contestation
and deconstruction, so that every person ensnared by it might
be liberated from unbearable bondage.

Chapter 2, "Man, the Lonely Animal," seemed to me then,
as now, the best way to address the arc of this historical development, which produces such anxiety, and provides no
easy answers—both here and in the Middle East. By way of
summary of the problem, from the vantage point of the aristocratic soul, the truant's freedom offered by the democratic
age is initially both temptation and horror. Once past a certain point in the transition to the democratic age, however,
attraction to aristocratic social conditions no longer holds the
heart and mind firm; now *repulsion* to aristocratic social conditions overrides the attraction. The unambiguous desire to
destroy any and all vestiges of the old order, so as to be "free,"
captivates the heart and mind. To make matters worse, the
impulse to destroy *increases* in proportion as there is less of
the aristocratic social order left to destroy. Here is the French
Revolutionary—and later the Marxist, and in our own day,
the identity politics zealot who also seems intent, to invoke
Marx's apt phrase, to "abolish the current state of things," and
yet who seems unaware of the immense destruction that his
movement *already* has caused. Delinked in a manner that is
historically unimaginable, here is a soul who is only *momen-
tarily rescued* from the loneliness that is its lot, by the fugitive
hope that if just a bit more debris from the old aristocratic social order can be blasted out of the way, the path home to The
Universal Brotherhood of Man, or The End of Alienation, or
in our own day, The End of Whiteness, will emerge into view.
As the reader will discover, my conclusion was that my Middle Eastern students generally locate themselves in the aristocratic configuration of being both attracted and repulsed
by the truant's freedom Tocqueville thought so dangerous.
My general conclusion was that many of my American students back in 2012 had already started to make the turn, so to

speak, and were heading toward the revolutionary frame of mind we now call identity politics, which seeks to undo anything that remains of our American inheritance. Anxiety was the common denominator for both groups of students; the unworkable answer to which my Middle Eastern students capitulated involved oscillating back and forth between aristocratic longings to return to an only-imagined past, and then rushing headlong into a hyper-modern future; the unworkable answer my American students held dear involved completing the deconstruction that was already well underway. If careful readers of that chapter discern a greater sympathy for the still somewhat embodied lives my Middle Eastern students possessed, they will not be off the mark. In this regard, I confess that what sometimes appeared as a description *of* my students in the Middle East was, in fact, more of a prescription *for* my American students at home. Not all of my American students wished deconstruction, of course. America today is, in fact, split down the middle between those who long for the release from the historical inheritances that would make them citizens of *this* nation, with *this* history, with *this* sort of family, with *this* religion, etc., and those who want to preserve and revitalize just those inheritances—not because they are pure, but because they are theirs. Here, I suppose, are the populists, though I think this a needlessly condescending term for the sort of life—namely, an embodied life—Tocqueville thought without which we would perish. The fateful struggle today is between those who wish for embodiment, and those who wish to flee from it.

In the intervening ten years, a great deal has happened in America, much of it involving the further working out of the longing for the disembodied cosmopolitan life about which Tocqueville so worried. The most important flash point for that longing today involves the escalating battle, which I suspect will be the most formidable issue of the 2024 Presidential campaign, over whether the categories of "man" and "woman" are natural or artificial social constructions. Tocqueville predicted that in the democratic age, we would become quite confused about these two categories—a development whose outlines I traced in the chapter on loneliness. He thought the heretofore uncontested natural differences between men and women would be subject first to doubt and then to vitriolic attack. Democratic man wants equality, and nothing, not even obdurate nature, will be permitted to stand in the way. The natural difference captured by the term "sex" would become an embarrassment, and be eagerly replaced by the fancy that the distinction is a merely socially constituted difference. In our own day we have invented a term that expresses that fancy, namely, "gender," which I think we would do well to jettison altogether. We probably should have understood at the time when the term "gender" came along, that that would not be the end of the matter. In a "gendered" world, not only are man and woman *interchangeable* categories, they are categories that can be remade, even rejected altogether, as they now increasingly are by a younger generation that has been taught that mankind is a cancer for which sexual regeneration is the accelerant, and for which neutering, death, or transhumanism, for some or all, is the cure. Tocqueville did not directly predict what we confront today, but what he did predict was the impending Great Democratic Exhaustion. Transgenderism, transhumanism, and let us add, the purported impending collapse of the "climate" unless we stop drilling for oil and start strip-mining for lithium and rare earth minerals, are all instances of this democratic exhaustion, which seeks purity or annihilation—*anything* except living in the coarse but workable world of people and things that actually surrounds us. These developments, needless to say, are unthinkable for aristocratic, embodied man. I suspect the chasm between the two self-understandings—that embodiment is to be rejected and that embodiment is to be embraced—will only further widen in the near future. The near future, it seems to me, is going to involve skirmishes and overt, clarifying battles over this fateful question, whose root cause is man's inability to contend with his experience of loneliness. Anyone who tells you otherwise is not paying attention. In loneliness, the stark alternatives are laid bare before us: communion or annihilation. It is not clear which of the two we will choose.

Chapter 3, "The Household: Sustenance and Reproduction," is oddly positioned between Chapter 2's examination of the experience of loneliness and Chapter 4's discussion of religion, which is to say the experience of *communion*. What does the household have to do with these sublime and intimate issues? The household—the *oikos*, the economy—is generally understood in a straightforward way, as pertaining to preferences and the rules necessary to secure and signal those preferences to others participating in a market. What has this exchange of *things* to do with the emptiness of loneliness that no *thing* can remedy, or the religious communion to which no *thing* can contribute? I sought in Chapter 3 to consider a question that anyone who attends to Tocqueville's thinking about democratic and aristocratic man will plainly understand, yet about which economic science has nothing to say, because it does not distinguish between honor culture, failure culture, and equality culture. For markets to work, failure must be an option; malinvestment must be cleared. Aristocratic societies are honor cultures, however; for members of such societies, failure does not prove that markets work, failure assaults the basic tenet of an aristocratic society: Face-saving must always be available. That is why aristocratic societies will *always* be suspicious of markets. The Anglo-American world, as Tocqueville pointed out, did not share this prejudice. Bankruptcies happen in America all the time, he noted. Democratic man is quite at home in a failure culture. Because malinvestment clears, capital can be rapidly reallocated to more productive use, which yields improvement. This, in turn, reduces the anxiety democratic man has about falling behind. This picture suggests that democratic man has a clear advantage over aristocratic man when it comes to markets. That is not the end of the matter, however. Democratic man also longs for equality.

This longing runs headlong into the iron-clad requirement in a failure culture that distinctions be made. Everyone does not get an "A." Everyone does not get a trophy. In America today, they do. Because of this, I suggested that the household, broadly understood, was not in great shape. Aristocratic societies were going to be reluctant to adopt failure culture, and so they will end up with choreographed economic activity that benefits a few chosen families or corporations; democratic societies, which *should* endorse failure culture, are choosing equality culture instead, and so real improvement is grinding to a halt. I have said this more clearly here, but the general outline of the argument was intact in the original. As of this writing, the top-down, low-risk, honor culture, aristocratic command-economies—notably China—have combined with the currently ruling elites in the Anglo-American world (the "globalists") who are committed to equality culture and the top-down organization that it entails. Neither group wants the failure culture necessary for real improvement, which would put them out of business. We will see if this configuration can last. I doubt it can. Speaking biblically, for a moment, no Tower of Babel construction of man has ever endured. God's plans exceed man's plans. Always. It is not a question of whether the global edifice held together in one half of the globe by aristocratic honor culture and in the other half by democratic equality culture will collapse; the question is when, and by what causes.

Of all the chapters in *Tocqueville in Arabia*, Chapter 4, "Religion," has most perplexed readers. Tocqueville wrote a great deal about the need for religion in the democratic age, and went so far as to argue that, without it, democratic man will fall into tyranny—the "equality of all in servitude," he called it. In a book concerned with the anxiety of the democratic age, the subject of religion, therefore, cannot be avoided. Tocqueville's treatment of the matter concerned the healthy habits of mind Christianity inculcated, and the experience of suffering he thought Christianity was best equipped to console. What is missing in the whole of *Democracy in America* is an exposition of the Christian understanding of sin and redemption, which I thought necessary to rehearse for my Middle Eastern students who are perplexed or horrified by the idea of original sin and an Incarnate God, and for my nominally Christian students in America whose religious understanding is deformed or absent altogether. I will say more about this shortly, but first, a comment on religion in the democratic age.

Both Christianity and Islam are in a dis-eased state these days. Each came into being, so to speak, during the aristocratic age. Each is therefore a ragged survivor, compelled to adjust to, or resist, the sentiments and sensibilities that emerge in the democratic age. Most notably, each is faced with a perennial crisis of authority, which Tocqueville thought would ravage all of our institutions in the democratic age, not least our religious ones. Who speaks *for* Islam? The imams in Saudi Arabia, Egypt, Turkey, or Iran? It is not clear. Who speaks *for* Christianity? The Reformation and the Treaty of Westphalia put an end to any uncontested answer in Europe and in the Anglo-sphere.

With regard to Islam, the problem that lies ahead is the one it has contended with for centuries, namely, what is its relationship to what we are here calling the democratic age, or what others might call "modernity"? No one really has an answer: Some insist on "going back," though it is not clear what that would entail; some are choosing to be culturally Muslim in the democratic age and abandoning strict religious adherence; and some are giving up on Islam altogether. I doubt Islam is going to die. When religions die, the civilizations that carry them die as well. That is not going to happen in the Middle East. The view I expressed in *Tocqueville in Arabia*, which I still hold, is that Islam will begin to recover its bearings not as a transnational *Umma*, but rather through constitutional monarchies within the nation-state system, the latter of which I take to be an accomplished and irrevocable fact of the international order.

With regard to Christianity in the democratic age, the question is not whether it can survive, but whether it has lost sight of the somber judgmental God, and gone *all in* for the God of love, who accepts and loves man "just the way he is"—which is to say, self-satisfied, prideful, full of himself, and lost to himself. Prior to when the "dogma of equality" (Tocqueville's term) took hold, the God of Christianity extended mercy to all, but adjudged that some would spend eternity in hell. In the democratic age, however, man wants universal salvation. Everyone gets a trophy, in this life and in the next. Judgment is out; love and mercy are in. God goes soft, and so do the churches.

This development has made it very difficult for both my Muslim students in the Middle East and my nominally Christian students in America to understand the distinctly Christian claim about the *need* for an Incarnate God. This is not the place to rehearse that argument in detail. I only pause to note that there would have been no *need* for God to send Himself in incarnate form had Adam not radically turned away from Him. Original sin and the Incarnate God *go together*.

Here, however, I want to briefly alert the reader to the consequences of abandoning the God who judges man's sin, and choosing the God of love alone instead. When the churches in the democratic age abandoned the God of Judgment, as they largely did as the twentieth century wore on, the idea of irredeemable sin disappeared in the churches, but it did not disappear altogether. Irredeemable sin became political. Today, in the Democratic Party, a new political religion has full command over the hearts and minds of elect parishioners, who operate on the basis of an intersectional debt-point scheme that gives them moral clarity about who is pure and who is stained. This is identity politics, the spiritual eugenics of our time. When I wrote *Tocqueville in Arabia* a decade ago, I worried that Christianity was becoming incoherent, because it was losing sight of the necessary co-relationship between original sin and the Incarnate God. Today, I worry that the idea of original sin has migrated out of the churches and into politics, there to take the form of identity politics group-scapegoating, which intends to purge those who are irredeemably stained, along with all that they have wrought in history, so that the world may be made pure. Can this migration into politics of the Christian idea of original sin last? I do not think so, though how and why this maddening heresy ends remains unclear. My assessment of the phenomenon as a whole can be found in *American Awakening: Identity Politics and Other Afflictions of Our Time.* I made no mention of identity politics in *Tocqueville in Arabia.* I did see, however, that the failure of Christians to understand the centrality of the idea of original sin in their religion was already a problem.

Finally, I owe the reader an account of why *Tocqueville in Arabia* takes the mixed form of autobiography and political theory. Why not just write political theory? I count it an incalculable blessing that I did my graduate training at the University of Chicago, in the mid-1980s, under the last generation of scholars who lived in close proximity to World War II. That generation posed for itself the question: What do the Great Books tell us about the civilizational collapse that had almost just occurred? Their correlative method, so to speak, of moving seamlessly between the canon of Great Books and the near catastrophe they had lived through *was* political theory. That method distinguished it from the sort of inquiry undertaken in Philosophy Departments and in History Departments. As decade followed decade, political theory has lost sight of this methodical charge, and has become increasingly irrelevant as a consequence. Political theory today more involves attending to the mind-numbing secondary and tertiary "literature." Feeling under a considerable obligation to reinstate the method of relying on the Great Books to illuminate the agonizing events of our time, I wrote *Tocqueville in Arabia.* The Middle East is in agony. So, too, is America. I doubt we are going to be able to understand either unless we turn to the Great Books for guidance. Tocqueville's *Democ-*

racy in America is one of those guides. Perhaps the best one. But let us not also not forget the corollary insight: Unless we ask of the Great Books that they illuminate the anxieties and agony of our time, they are but black ink on white paper, of no use to anyone.

Preface to the 2013 Edition

For five of the past seven years, I have been in the Middle East—three in Qatar, helping Georgetown establish its School of Foreign Service there; and two in Iraq, helping to build the nascent American University of Iraq, Sulaimani. *Tocqueville in Arabia* pertains to the three years I spent in Qatar, between 2005 and 2008. In the course of my overseas duties, there was one author whom I carried with me daily. Indeed, not an hour went by when Tocqueville's thinking about the movement from the aristocratic age to the democratic age did not occupy my imagination.

Now, seven years later, my conclusions—or, rather, my premonitions, apprehensions, and hopes—have been drawn together in *Tocqueville in Arabia*, a work whose ancient ancestry might be Montesquieu's *Persian Letters*, and whose recent pedigree might be traced to an imagined embrace between Azar Nafisi's *Reading Lolita in Tehran* and Allan Bloom's *The Closing of the American Mind*. Like Nafisi's work, *Tocqueville in Arabia* seeks to illuminate the concerns of students in the distant lands of the Middle East; like Bloom's work, it aspires to be a comprehensive reflection on the challenges facing America today. I hasten to add that where Bloom saw America through the lens of Rousseau's suspicions of the modern world, I have fixed my gaze on Tocqueville, who understood that modernity—the democratic age, in his terms—is here to stay; and that our charge is to reinforce its strengths and be mindful of its weaknesses.

Tocqueville in Arabia is in one sense a work of political theory—how could I escape that? Yet after having written several rather formal works in political theory, it seemed to me that to understand what I was witnessing in the Middle East, a different sort of book needed to be written, one that always returned to the evidence—in this case, the years of discussions I have had with my students in the Middle East and on the main campus here at Georgetown. These conversations led me again and again to wonder just how my students have arrived at the conclusions they hold. Throughout *Tocqueville in Arabia* my answer has been twofold: on the one hand, the students have been shaped by the understandings and misunderstandings of the sixties generation and, just as importantly, by the longer trends associated with the developments of the democratic age itself. This twofold answer has necessitated that I weave occasional reflections about the 1960s into the larger theoretical argument on which I rely, which can be found on nearly every page of *Democracy in America*, Alexis de Tocqueville's magisterial work. The result, as I have mentioned, is a book that is both less and more than a conventional work of political theory. I will leave it to the reader to decide if there is something to be gained by writing in this way.

In *Tocqueville in Arabia*, I have sought at once to be generous and critical of developments happening in the Middle East and in America. Some will say I have gone too far, and some will say that I have not gone far enough. Above all, I have sought to foster an understanding about one another that eludes Americans and Middle Easterners alike. The need to undertake this task I take to be self-evident. Yet where today can the earnest reader discover how such understanding might be achieved? The daily media reports are scarcely helpful. Polemicists on both sides tend to deepen the existing wounds. And scholars, in general, speak only to one another, in a language that the earnest reader finds tedious, unhelpful, or arcane. Clearly a new kind of writing is needed to help bring about the understanding that is sorely lacking.

Before beginning in earnest, something needs to be said here about a more traditional convention of writing that I have used throughout *Tocqueville in Arabia*. It goes without saying that in the age of equality, the use of the term "man" is likely to be jarring. Indeed, Tocqueville himself gives us the reason why this is likely to be so: as conditions become more equal, we are apt to become uncomfortable with terms that seem exclusionary. Unity, Tocqueville says, becomes an obsession. And so it is not surprising that the once-conventional term "man" falls out of favor in the democratic age. The difficulty faced by the contemporary writer who wishes to maintain fidelity with a great author who writes before these new conventions arose is, therefore, formidable. Tocqueville's use of the term "man" is ubiquitous. Indeed, some of the most powerful and eloquent passages in *Democracy in America* involve the term "man." Not wishing to alter his usage when I cite passages from his writing, I thought it best to maintain consistency throughout *Tocqueville in Arabia* and use his term "man." To readers unaccustomed or uncomfortable with this older convention, I ask that they indulge my interest that parsimony be maintained, and that they look beyond the form of my writing to the content itself. My hope is that they will be rewarded by doing so. The matter is made more complicated, as the reader soon will discover, because on many occasions I use the terms "fathers," "mothers," "sons," and "daughters." Tocqueville worried that in the democratic age, the great temptation would be to think only about the present moment and lose sight of the fact that society must be in the business of regenerating itself. My invocation of the terms "fathers," "mothers," "sons," and "daughters" occurs in those places when such regeneration is directly at issue or lurking in the background. Critics will point out that there is something to be gained by avoiding these various usages; I have thought it necessary, however, to rely on these archaisms so that certain issues can be illuminated that otherwise might remain obscure.

A final word that prepares the way for all that follows. In the "Author's Introduction" to *Democracy in America*, published in 1833, Tocqueville wrote, "I have tried to see not differently but further than any party; while they are busy with tomorrow, I have wished to consider the whole future." *Tocqueville in Arabia* seeks to take the measure of his distant and prophetic vision, by aligning it with the thoughts and sentiments that prevail in the minds and hearts of my students, in the troubled and terrible age that is now upon us.

Prologue

Fathers and Sons

Not long after I arrived in Qatar in the fall of 2005, I was introduced to a Saudi Arabian man roughly my age, over coffee at a local café. His English was impeccable. I did not ask but gathered that the ease with which he spoke came from years spent in the United States as a college student, something a great many young men from the Gulf region have done for over a generation. He also had that certain sophistication that invariably comes from time spent in Europe. His clothing, the way he carried himself, an aloofness that announced a rank and pedigree that in America have all but been eliminated—here was a man familiar with three worlds, intertwined yet on still different courses. A Saudi Arabian by birth, I intimated that he had seen too much of the world beyond its borders to have been able to return home with his allegiance intact, but not enough of America and Europe to find enduring comfort there either.

We exchanged pleasantries for nearly an hour, commented on how quickly Qatar was entering the modern world, and expressed relief that late afternoon temperatures had finally dropped to the upper nineties. Then, looking up from the coffee cup he had carefully encircled with both hands, he said to me with some urgency, "You must understand what happened to my generation in some parts of the Arab world. You speak in America of 'the sixties generation.' Do not forget that Europe also had its sixties generation, and so did we. In America, there was rock-and-roll and social experimentation;

young people lost their way with drugs and repudiated the authority of their fathers. African Americans laid claim to rights that had long been overdue, and women renounced their place in the home granted to them by nature and by tradition. Yes, there was great experimentation—and a great many mistakes. Yet when you finally began to settle down, your habits of experimentation, your doubt about the authority of the past, and your boldness of thought led to unheralded innovations in technology and to practical applications in everyday life that brought an explosion in the standard of living of the sort that the world has never seen."

"In Europe," he continued, "the sixties generation was no less contemptuous of their fathers, for they had nearly destroyed their nations with war and brought shame upon the continent. In America, you have a think tank called the Heritage Foundation, yes? Can you imagine a German think tank with that name? It cannot be done. The heritage of Europe in the twentieth century brought no pride to the sixties generation there. And so while you labored to build your world through innovation and experimentation, in Europe the sixties generation labored to extend the modest beginnings of European integration that began in 1951 with the creation of the European Coal and Steel Community, with a view to establishing a fully integrated European Union, a transpolitical entity by which the sons said to their fathers: 'We will never allow the shame that two World Wars brought our nations to happen again.' That will be their legacy, as innovation and productive advancement will be yours."

The tone of his voice now became strained. "In Saudi Arabia, we, too, had our sixties generation. And we, too, very much had our fathers on our mind. In our eyes, our fathers had made a devil's bargain with 'the West.' Unwilling to share power or to encourage growth, however, they settled down halfway between the grand past of the Muslim age and a modern life that we saw on our televisions but never in our homes or in our cities. Hostile to what this troubling compromise had brought, our religious teachers told us that the world could only be made whole by returning to the pure teachings of Islam. And because nothing occurs without the sanction of religious men in our country, we listened. 'Our politics are corrupt,' we cried. 'Islam is the solution,' they responded. 'Global commerce holds out many promises, but we see only a caricature of its benefits,' we declared. 'Islam is the solution,' they replied. 'In America and in Europe, women have broken free of the household,' we told them. 'Islam is the solution,' they proclaimed. For every stress and strain of modern life, our elders had but one answer: 'Islam.' Islam would allow us to overcome the shame brought upon us by our fathers' halfway capitulation to 'the West.' Or so we came to believe. So while your sixties generation was innovating and building a world, while Europe's sixties generation was creating the European Union, ours was dreaming of a pristine Islamic world and how we might bring it about. Do not forget, when you speak of the sixties generation, that yours was not the only one, that each of us threw off our fathers: in America, it has turned out well; in Europe, the verdict is not yet in; in the Arab world, confusion has deepened into despair."

Interested in the history of ideas, and knowing that I had come to Qatar to be a member of the start-up team for Georgetown's nascent School of Foreign Service there, he wondered what would bring an American to the Gulf for several years to teach the history of Western political thought to a population of mostly Muslim students. I told him that I had been chairman of the Department of Government at Georgetown's main campus for the previous three years, and despite my recent reelection to a second term as chairman, I had jumped without hesitation at the opportunity to teach in the Middle East.

"The university," I said, "is the only institution in the known universe dedicated to the love of truth and to the civil discussion of ideas. That love and civility is to be found in the classroom, however, not in the office of an academic departmental chair. And so, to the classroom I am returning." He laughed, congratulated me on being heir to a grand tradition that may yet play a conciliatory role in this already deeply troubled century, and then was on his way.

I sat quietly for another hour or so, as the temperature dropped and the sun set without announcement, and pondered the more personal sense in which my arrival in the Middle East involved a return, which I did not convey that afternoon over coffee—for in the Middle East, friendship and its confidences are not won in a single meeting. Anyone whose formative years have been spent abroad and who subsequently comes to America never has an easy time figuring out where home truly lies. The passage of time only partly erases the discomfort. The résumé of mine begins in Cairo, where I was born while my father was doing his doctoral research on the Muslim Brotherhood—the group without which Al-Qaeda and other kindred groups would not have taken the form they have today.

My connection to Cairo is made more complicated by the fact that in 1983, at the age of twenty-eight, I returned there in an unsuccessful attempt to bring my father home to the States after he underwent emergency surgery for the cancer that his doctors in Ann Arbor had failed to detect. In his hospital room for a week, I watched helplessly as his life slowly ebbed away, marveling at one moment at the tenacity and at another at the frailty of our mortal frame. Then, in what would be a final heroic effort to stem the internal bleeding, his doctors opted for a second surgery. As he was being wheeled toward the operating room, his hand felt exhausted and weak in mine, as if whatever strength he had left was being held in reserve for one last undertaking. Just before the doors opened, we looked into each other's eyes and without a word from his lips I understood him to say, "This is the end, son; we will not see each other again on this side of life's curtain. What you have inherited from me you will understand in the years to come." He died that afternoon in the city he both adored and loved to hate. As I flew out of Cairo the following evening, I peered out the airplane window into the yellow nightglow of the pyramids below. With tears in my eyes, I vowed that I would never return to the city of my birth or to any other city in the Middle East.

It is not Cairo, however, that is indelibly fixed in my memory. During my formative years, I lived in countries that most of my American friends did not know even existed until two decades ago: Kuwait and Yemen. It is always difficult to reconstruct the memories of one's youth, since fact and fiction intermingle, and in hindsight the angle of events seems less acute. My father had emerged from World War II, like so many other veterans, with a grand optimism that the world could be made a far better place than the one he had witnessed. A decade and a half later, with a PhD from Princeton in hand, he found himself a representative of the United States government, in a region of the world he knew through long nights of study, and by the fortune of family lineage, the latter serving him as a sort of intuitive compass during his years at Princeton and beyond. In Yemen, my father and another State Department colleague were the first officials to represent the United States government, a fact that so irritated the Soviets they suggested to Yemeni officials that my father and his colleague might be members of the American intelligence community. Some six months into our stay, we were given twenty-four hours to burn our documents and leave the country. I departed with dim but durable memories of lazy, bumpy treks along steep mountain paths, securely snuggled next to my four-year-old twin sister in a saddle on the back of a donkey, escorted by kind but impoverished guides, in whom my parents had unwavering trust. It was the 1950s, the era of martinis and Kent cigarettes, when United States citizenship brought honor — and more than a little envy too — in a world still emerging from the vast destruction of a global war.

The Kuwait of my youth was not without a measure of quiet

stability. Our life was sheltered by compound walls, beyond which was a vast ocean of sand into which new roads to the embassy had to be cut each time we ventured forth. Beyond this shimmering granular ocean lay the Persian Gulf, where we would spend hour after spectacular hour bodysurfing on waves that broke gently on beaches that seemed to stretch without interruption to the even more mysterious lands without names to the south. Thirty-five years ago, I returned in search of a past I thought could be retrieved, or at least confirmed, only to discover that fifty-story skyscrapers now occupied my beaches. I have not gone back again.

After our two-year stay in Kuwait, my father accepted a position as a professor of modern Middle Eastern history, at the University of Michigan in Ann Arbor. The year 1963 was a momentous one in the United States, confusing to those firmly interwoven into its social fabric, bewildering to a little boy of eight who still dreamed in Arabic, and who had no firm recollection of a country that was his own by law but foreign by any other measure. My father's book *The Society of the Muslim Brothers*, so long in the making, was published in 1969, in no small part because his doctoral advisors—and at times even he—did not believe that Islam of any persuasion could withstand the overriding power and logic of modernization. That was, of course, two years after yet another great Arab-Israeli war, the Six-Day War of June 1967. While I dimly recall my father talking about any number of public debates in which he participated at that time (and also during the 1973 war), my only vivid recollections are of packed meetings at the university's Hillel House, the local Jewish community center, in Ann Arbor, where whatever convergence of the minds that had occurred between the two sides was always brought to an abrupt halt by the testimony of a teary-eyed survivor of the Holocaust. There is, properly speaking, no possible response to such testimony, since its warrant to authority was the horror of the event itself. My father knew this but sought, without success, to find a way to hold together the two ineluctable facts about the region: Israel was here to stay; and the Palestinians could not be ignored.

During those years in Ann Arbor, my father would frequently travel back to the Middle East and return with artifacts whose scent and touch would transport my sister and me to the distant lands we had once known so well. Yet aside from a winter spent in Cairo in 1976, a summer spent working in Saudi Arabia in 1978, and, as I mentioned, the brief but unsuccessful trip to Cairo in 1983 to try to bring my father home alive, I had no real interest in returning to the Middle East to live for an extended period. That was my father's world, not mine. I had made my peace with becoming a midwesterner. No life, after all, is without its fragments that do not fit neatly together. That mine took the form it did—the sun-scorched Arabian Peninsula and the quiet, elm tree–lined streets of Ann Arbor, without a common denominator between them— is something the passage of time had made less painful, not unlike the mercy the passage of time grants to love's once-aching wounds.

Recollections

On the afternoon of September 10, 2001, in Alexandria, Virginia, not more than three miles from the Pentagon, I sat talking with my eldest son about his generation and about mine. Then sixteen years old, he dimly understood the facts that had formed my generation without knowing how they affected the interior life of those who bore witness to them.

I told him about my mother's horror at having brought my younger brother home from Sibley Memorial Hospital in Washington, DC, two days before President Kennedy's proclamation to Cuba and to the Soviet Union on October 22, 1962: "It shall be the policy of this nation to regard any nuclear missile launched from Cuba against any nation in the Western Hemisphere as an attack on the United States, requiring a full retaliatory response upon the Soviet Union." And as I recounted the event, I wondered how I would have reacted if the world had been brought to the brink of nuclear annihilation two days after either of my sons had come into the world.

I told him about our move to Ann Arbor in the summer of 1963 and about that awful rainy afternoon of November 22, when I raced breathlessly into the house upon hearing the news on the playground down the street that President Kennedy had been shot in Dallas; and how I found my mother weeping in front of the twelve-inch black-and-white television set in the darkened living room, holding out hope until Walter Cronkite—America's unofficial anchorman—fumbled to remove his thick, black-rimmed glasses and announced, with broken voice and an only partially concealed tear, that John F. Kennedy was dead.

I told him about how Martin Luther King, the prophetic voice not only of the disenfranchised descendants of America's ignominious experiment with slavery but of the nation as a whole, called on America to fulfill what Providence had written on the human heart: that men and women were to be judged "not by the color of their skin, but by the content of their character." I told him of our anguish upon hearing that he had been shot and killed that unsuspecting spring evening of April 4, 1968, in Memphis; and how the grandeur of his life was belied by the place of his assassination: on a balcony overlooking a motel parking lot—in an ancillary place in American life, not unlike the ancillary place to which the American Negro (my son was notably awkward at my utterance of the word) had been relegated for centuries. I told him of how night after night cities across America were set ablaze, and of how school cafeterias and hallways in the Ann Arbor public schools were suddenly filled with armed policemen instead of overzealous functionaries whose paltry task it had been to assure that the relatively innocent crime of skipping class did not go unpunished.

I told him of how, as spring became summer in that momentous year of 1968, we held our breath in the hope that Robert

Kennedy's run for the Democratic Party nomination might restore America's footing; and of how my mother, by now nearly numb from two previous assassinations, stirred us from our slumber on the morning of June 6, with word that he, too, had been shot and killed the night before in Los Angeles, amidst the celebration of his victory in the California Democratic Primary. Her quivering tone was one of incredulity and resignation. Had she not adjudged the Methodist Church of her youth to be a necessary casualty of her unlikely admission to Vassar College from the small town of Wheeler, Indiana, two decades earlier, I imagine her words might have been, "How much more suffering, oh God of mercy and hope, must we endure?" Without compass, I graduated from the seventh grade twelve days later.

I told him of our trip east in August 1968 in our gray Peugeot station wagon, listening to CKLW, the legendary 50,000-watt AM radio station broadcasting from Windsor, Ontario. Without seat belts to restrain us, singing songs of love and protest, windows wide open, the dog ecstatic over the new scents that overtook her with each passing mile, we were blithely oblivious that the protection our music offered against an unraveling world was as frail as that offered by our wispy Peugeot traveling along US 80 at high speed. Arriving in Waterford, Connecticut, at a favorite aunt's house, we spent days by the ocean, alternating between the tidal pools whose wonders I could understand and the beaches whose wonders a thirteen-year-old boy could not possibly fathom.

The innocence of those daily excursions to the beach, I told him, was overshadowed by the Democratic National Convention, held in Chicago, from August 26 to 29. On those steamy evenings, with fans whirling in the background but doing little good, we watched the Democratic Party of the New Deal succumb, as much because of what was happening inside the convention as was happening outside, in Grant and Lincoln Parks, where a new Democratic Party was coalescing. Hubert Horatio Humphrey, a stalwart of the New Deal, won the formal endorsement of a now-unraveling party coalition held together by blue-collar workers, moderate southerners, old-line Progressives, and ethnic immigrants, intent on providing a better life for their children. Humphrey's acceptance speech was gracious and, at times, moving; but it was Eugene McCarthy's speech in Grant Park that began to consolidate the views of the new Democratic Party, the party of 1968. Suspicious that all wars are imperial adventures; dubious that corporations contribute much to the national good; adamant that race, class, and gender are the only considerations to be brought to bear when thinking about justice; and skeptical that religion is anything more than false-consciousness—the party of 1968 that rallied on the grounds of those Chicago parks dedicated to Presidents Lincoln and Grant during the sweltering nights of late August spurned its historical constituencies and set the stage for the 1980 Reagan Revolution, from which the Democratic Party has never fully recovered.

I told him that as I watched angry young men only a few years older than me clash with police in Chicago in 1968—and again in 1969, a few blocks from our house in Ann Arbor, between June 16 and 19—I realized a chasm would always separate those who underwent the gauntlet of the Vietnam draft and those who did not. That gauntlet had been no less effective at distinguishing men from boys than would have been a primitive tribal initiation rite. My only palpable exposure to that war would come in the form of news that the elder brother of a friend had just died half a world away, or an awkward moment at a junior high school party, where I would stutter and stammer words of consolation that were woefully inadequate to the task.

I told him that I learned of the outbreak of the Ann Arbor riots of 1969 when my father walked home from campus that Monday afternoon, June 16, visibly enraged, and announced that "the students have cordoned off South University and are fornicating in the streets." To which he added quickly, "And I forbid you to go up there." I did sneak out of the house later that night after my father and mother had gone to sleep, to survey the carnage. Having delivered newspapers in the neighborhood, I knew the shortcuts and alleys that would hide me from notice. Not knowing what to expect, my imagination wandered. Safely hidden in the bushes next to the Engineering School, I watched as long-haired college students taunted Sheriff Harvey's black-leather-clad police officers by inserting daisies into the barrels of their shotguns. The entire scene was a parody of itself, both sides knowing in advance the part they were to play. I went home knowing how the rest of the script would play out. And it did, during the remaining days of the Ann Arbor standoff and during the many college campus protests around the country that followed—until the script was finally thrown out on May 4, 1970, at Kent State University.

As I walked through our back gate on Olivia Street, I paused in the solitude of our backyard, where partly to show my solidarity with the dawning environmental movement and partly because I was consigned to cut the grass with a hand-mower, I had transformed a well-manicured lawn into a modest forest of white pine and red oak saplings. Nature seemed to offer the only place of repose during those turbulent times. Little wonder that Ansel Adams posters—*El Capitan, Winter, Moon Over Half Dome, Winter Sunrise, Sierra Nevada*—decorated the walls of bedrooms and dorm rooms around the country.

I told my son of how we held our breath on July 16, 1969, as we watched the first-stage engines of *Apollo 11*, with their seven and a half million pounds of thrust, groan to life and hurl six million pounds of rocket gracefully skyward, along with the dreams of a nation exhausted by its tribulations—a spectacle that was outdone by the blurry but discernible image of Neil Armstrong and Buzz Aldrin walking on the surface of the moon four days later, early on the morning of July 20, 1969. The Ansel Adams who will depict the lunarscape to my grandchildren has perhaps already been born.

I told him of yet another trip east in our Peugeot station wagon that same year, in August 1969, and of how during our several-day meanderings through New York State, we paused to consider whether we might stop along the way and attend a set or two at a three-day concert held in Bethel, between August 15 and 18; but decided against it more than a hundred miles away because of the snarl of traffic. That was Woodstock.

I told him that his generation was unlike mine because his generation lacked a set of events that defined it. We all went quietly to sleep that night, and the next morning my son's generation found its event, and the world I had more or less put to rest long ago awoke and began to reemerge into the bright light of day.

1 *Colliding and Converging Worlds*

Discovering Tocqueville

A book with the odd title *Tocqueville in Arabia* needs something of an explanation. Those of us who surround ourselves with great books as others surround themselves with friends never lack for good company. While I had read fragments of Tocqueville's *Democracy in America* in graduate school, the compression of course work, comprehensive exams, and the inordinate focus of dissertation writing allowed me to conclude my studies at the University of Chicago in 1989 with a doctorate in political science without ever having read that magisterial work in its entirety. The following year, with two children under the age of five, a Hyde Park rent to pay, and no tenure-track job in sight, I accepted a postdoc position teaching the important ideas of social science and psychology in the University of Chicago's Common Core, for the demoralizing salary of $12,000. In preparation for one of the courses I was to offer, I trundled off to Regenstein Library with *Democracy in America* in hand and began to read the "Author's Introduction," which was some twelve pages in length.

I do not recall how long I spent engrossed in those twelve pages. It might have been an hour; it might have been two or three. It did not matter; what I found there was beyond measure. As with friends, no less is true with great books: we know in an instant whether they are to be lifelong companions. When I finished and returned from my transfixed condition, I said to myself with certainty I have seldom known:

"You will spend the rest of your life with this book." The words were both recognition and command.

That certainty never left me. In 1990 I was able to secure a tenure-track position at the George Washington University, in no small measure, I was later told, because the search committee members concluded that notwithstanding my formal attire and somewhat arcane job talk, the Swatch watch I happened to be wearing that day gave them some confidence that dusty books were not my only friends. By day I was a teacher. By night I was an alchemist intent on transmuting the leaden weight of a dissertation into the gold of a publishable book manuscript, which I did in 1993 under the title *Not by Reason Alone*. But even as I tinkered with the formula for how to demonstrate that sixteenth-century Reformation categories suffused early modern political thought, I had already moved into the nineteenth-century world about which Tocqueville was writing, the proof of which was the growing number of interesting but probably superfluous footnotes about Tocqueville that appeared in *Not by Reason Alone* as I neared the completion of that thought experiment. Upon its publication, I turned my attention fully to Tocqueville's *Democracy in America*.

It is well to remember that America in the early 1990s had entered uncharted territory. To be more precise, while all nations at all times are always in uncharted territory, the categories that had ordered the American understanding of the world since the end of the Second World War—"East vs. West," "free market vs. command economy," "liberal democracy vs. totalitarian rule"—were no longer the comfortably reliable guides that they once had been. The Soviet Union had fallen. The ghastly clarity of the Cold War was behind us. Now what? Politicians gloated; anyone attuned to the world that sloganeering cannot comprehend was more circumspect.

In the academy, I watched as many tenured Marxists cloaked themselves in new camouflage—some turning to Habermas, others to Arendt, many to Foucault, and not a few to Derrida for their adornment. The revolution had not materialized; the forces of darkness were more sinister than even Marx had imagined. All who moved in these new directions shared Marx's disdain for what can loosely be called the Anglo-American tradition of liberalism. To become a member of this new vanguard, it was necessary to express contemptuous words about America at faculty meetings, conferences, dinner parties, and, of course, in the classroom. The spectacle gave cause to wonder: Protected by a system of lifetime tenure, did not society pay a high cost when professors confuse freedom of thought with polite and sophisticated forms of condescension and belittlement that they defend under the seemingly benign banner of "critique"? There were moments, indeed, when it would have been easy to conclude that the tenure system should have been abolished long ago—except that the cost society pays when freedom of thought is not so protected is higher still.

Under the watchful eyes of this cadre of academics, Tocqueville did not fare well. During the Cold War, after all, Tocqueville had been invoked against Marxism by defenders of the Anglo-American world—a fact neither forgotten nor forgiven.

As if that weren't enough for his detractors, Tocqueville's reservations about the coming equality of men and women sealed his fate. Attempts to explain the complexity of his thinking on that matter would fall on deaf ears during classroom lectures and at academic conferences. It was simply not possible in a public setting to doubt the complete equality—indeed the sameness—of men and women. I might have fallen into despair had it not been for the young men and women who would come to my office after class and confess, with some embarrassment, that they thought Tocqueville was right: because the burden of reproduction falls disproportionately to women, the household in which it occurred ought to be somehow protected. My formulation of that claim in class was no doubt stilted; I had, after all, grown up as a member of the sixties generation and had only recently lost my self-assurance about its categories and conclusions. When my eldest son, to whom you have already been introduced, held a Barbie doll by the legs, bent her torso over, and made an imaginary gun out of her when he was three years old, I could no longer believe that boys and girls, men and women, were not definitively different. It was one thing, however, to understand that an idea was ill-founded, and quite another to find a replacement. Two decades ago when I taught them, I passed with some awkwardness over Tocqueville's passages about women; now my students and I labor over those passages, which offer tantalizing hints about our plight, but no more than that. More so than my own generation, many of my students believe that something has gone wrong, even if they can't yet say what it is. Impatient with what appear to be hopelessly time-bound platitudes, they look upon many of my colleagues who disseminate them more as living artifacts of the late 1960s than as exemplars for the future.

At the other end of the political spectrum—which is to say, outside the academy, since conservatives of varying dispositions are only a hushed minority there—Tocqueville was no doubt respected, but I do not think he was well understood. Conservative thought in America has no single guiding principle; indeed, what unites conservatives is a suspicion of the very idea of governance by "principle." Place economic conservatives, social conservatives, libertarians, Protestant evangelicals, and conservative Roman Catholics in a colloquium together for three days, and you will soon discover the deep divisions among them. Disciplined on the airwaves by William F. Buckley and in print by Irving Kristol, and fortified on the ground by Ronald Reagan's political triumphs, conservatives were unified more by arguing with the Left than by agreeing among themselves. When threatened, they formed a circle and aimed their armaments outward. The Left formed a circle, too, but inflicted wounds on its own as often as not—until ever-expanding federal expenditures created the clientelist arrangements through which all of its constituencies could be sated.

From the outside, then, conservatives in the 1990s seemed unified; but from the inside, the crosscutting cleavages were painfully evident. Decorum could veil them, and political expediency could temporarily overcome them. The cleavages could not, however, be eliminated. Nowhere did these appear more clearly than in the assessment that conservatives offered of Tocqueville. Economic conservatives saw in him a basis for defending market commerce and rejecting administrative centralization; cultural conservatives saw in him the need to fortify family, local communities, and a legal system based on precedent; libertarians saw in him a defense of a minimalist state; Protestant evangelicals saw in him the claim that without Christianity the American polity would perish; conservative Roman Catholics saw in him a way to reconcile their faith with modernity. Tocqueville: a kaleidoscopic man for a kaleidoscopic coalition.

Against this backdrop, I turned my attention to Tocqueville in the early 1990s. It seemed to me then, as now, that the aspiration of Tocqueville's thought was more profound than Cold War partisans understood. "Left" and "Right" are, after all, terms that date from the French Legislative Assembly of 1791, which is to say to the aftermath of the French Revolution. Tocqueville took the measure of these terms without being implicated by them. His concern seemed deeper, more audacious, more prophetic and anticipatory: to explore and map an emerging psychological terrain, of which the French Revolution was but a résumé and a manifestation. "Democratic man," as Tocqueville called him, was a new type of man. Shorn of the social links that had once held him fast, he oscillated back and forth—now thinking himself capable of all things, now despairing of his insignificance; now throwing himself frantically into the world, now broodingly withdrawing. In short, democratic man was untethered man, in desperate need of salutary bondage, so as to protect him from himself.

Today we have concluded that this oscillation within the soul is a psychiatric "condition," which we have named "manic depression" or, more benignly, "bipolar disorder." Prior to the twentieth century, when man was thought to be more than the tracings of his brain chemistry, there were other accounts. Tocqueville's was that delinked, untethered man had to be *voluntarily* relinked—through civic associations, freely chosen marriage, freely chosen churches, and participation in local political life. Without these antidotes, he intimated, the democratic age would see an increase in madness and anxiety. Little wonder, then, that in America, the country where individuated, delinked man would prevail were there not palliatives, doctors of one sort prescribe drugs in the way that they do. Tocqueville's doctoring took a different form. Understanding that delinked man is a fragile creature, his prescription was to bring neighbor into proximity with neighbor, to ennoble the natural affection between a man and a woman within the confines of marriage, to remind mortal creatures that the unity God brings about is infinitely more fertile than any version man's imagination and action might contrive, and to encourage a modest politics in which all citizens can participate. Most importantly, Tocqueville sought amelioration, not cure; for he knew that man was an imperfect creature, whose dreams of a fugitive perfection can never see the light of day in this world below. With these insights in mind, and under the title *The Fragility of Freedom*, my first sustained exploration of Tocqueville came to a close in 1995.

Forays to Buenos Aires and Lisbon

I had by that time moved further up the Potomac River, to Georgetown University, where I still make my professional home, and through which I eventually had the opportunity to teach in Argentina for three consecutive summers, beginning in 2000. Buenos Aires is the most European of South American cities, a point of pride for many of its citizens and a source of irritation for much of the rest of Latin America. The European architecture that stands watch from the eighteenth and nineteenth centuries still sets the standard and the tone for much of what transpires there, from fashion to art to the life of the mind.

I quickly learned that as water spirals in the opposite direction in the Southern Hemisphere, so, too, the sentiments of most of my students in Buenos Aires were often diametrically opposed to those of my students on Georgetown's main campus in Washington, DC. Tocqueville was on the syllabus, of course, but the vagaries of the program in which I taught required that I focus on the history of political economy rather than the history of political thought. So, in addition to Tocqueville, we read a number of other eighteenth- and nineteenth-century luminaries—Jean-Jacques Rousseau, Adam Smith, Immanuel Kant, and Karl Marx—whom I took to be representative of an economic debate that had been recently settled.

I was mistaken.

In Washington, the end of the Cold War had meant that the long battle of ideas between Smith and Kant (who both believed in the gradual improvements wrought by commerce) and Rousseau and Marx (who were scandalized by this notion) ceased to be of interest to anyone but the historian and the archivist. This was not to say that the victory had settled all remaining questions: my students on Georgetown's main campus may have known that this view of commerce had won, but many were anxious about what it meant. It is true, of course, that some of them dreamed of an alternative—but only until graduation, after which point they were able to remember the difference between how the world *really* worked from how it ideally *might* work. Growing up in Ann Arbor in the 1960s, I quickly grasped the difference between the sometimes harsh realities of the playground and the platitudes our teachers got us to repeat but never fully believe in the classroom. I suspect that my students on Georgetown's main campus had learned the same lesson. America was a nation of traders, Tocqueville noted. It remains so today. Dream what they will, American students sooner or later come back to earth.

In Buenos Aires, a hemisphere away, things looked quite different: there, my students were suspicious of Smith and Kant even after having read them and were sympathetic to Rousseau and Marx without having read them at all. This was an anomaly that could not be explained away by some deficiency in their education. On the whole, my students there were far better educated than the students I had taught on Georgetown's main campus. In Buenos Aires, they wrestled less with the question of how to juxtapose commerce with other facets of life than with whether "commercial man" was anything other than an ideological pretense. The Cold War was over, yet Rousseau and Marx had lost none of their appeal. What, I wondered, allowed this to happen? What loud and resonant chord did these thinkers strike, such that a bad note here or there—say, the repudiation of Marxist economic thought— did not much disturb the ear that heard it?

For three years I flew back and forth between Washington summers and Buenos Aires winters pondering this question. During the days while my students worked, I would wander through the city until my lungs ached from the cold, damp air and the automobile exhaust. During our three-hour evening class sessions, my voice would ache from the labor of explaining ideas that my students evaluated by some supra-textual criteria I could never quite grasp. After our meetings, a number of us would often go out for long dinners, until midnight and beyond, where my heart would ache from the stories my students told me about how hard they worked and how little hope many of them held out for the future. In the early years of the twentieth century, the standard of living in the United States and in Argentina was roughly equivalent. It has increasingly diverged ever since. The last year I taught, the currency had recently been devalued and lower-middle-class families— fathers, mothers, sons, and daughters—could be seen on the streets late at night pushing shopping carts and looking for recycled materials they could collect and sell. And still the chord resounded.

Looking back on the first and second of my wondrous three interludes in Buenos Aires, I recall my students thinking that Tocqueville's *Democracy in America* was a book about and for Americans, those exceptional and curious people to the far north whose development shed little light either on what had happened in Argentina since the era of European colonialism or on what lay ahead for their future. I did nothing to dissuade them. I taught Tocqueville less as a protagonist or detractor in the debate about commerce than as someone who showed why commerce worked in America and, more importantly, why the romantic rejection of commerce (Rousseau) or the revolutionary aspiration to supersede its current "capitalist" form (Marx) had never widely captivated the American imagination. America: the exceptional case. In a short but provocative aside in *The Wealth of Nations*, Smith noted that nations with growing economies tend to be optimistic, whereas nations with declining economies tend to be melancholic. More than I was prepared to admit, I allowed that distinction to settle my perplexity about the difference between the beautiful souls I taught in Buenos Aires whose melancholy spiraled one way, and the pragmatic souls I taught in Washington whose interests spiraled in the opposite direction. So simple an account should not have satisfied me; but the sad fact about most of us is that having once triumphed over our initial confusion with whatever tools we proudly have at our disposal, we rest there contentedly as if no further work need be done.

Such self-satisfaction seldom lasts, however; something always eventually rousts us from our self-incurred slumber. In March 2002, just before my final excursion to Buenos Aires (in August of that year), I was asked to lecture on Tocqueville for several weeks in Portugal. More exactly, I lectured in Lisbon on the weekends and spent my weekdays far from the city, on small winding roads that never seemed to disturb the contours of a land bespeckled with grape vines and olive trees. Automobiles were newcomers here, and the very scale and placement of the roads announced that an enchanted past took precedent. Far from the bustle of Lisbon, here was a territory where ancient stone castles declared that novelty and improvement were not all that mattered.

In class back in Lisbon, I was surprised to discover that many of the sentiments that had become familiar to me during my sweater-clad days in Buenos Aires echoed here as well. Yet unlike Argentina, Portugal was a nation on the rise. Thanks to the European Union—with its grand postwar promise that burdensome national economic policy could be exchanged for both supra-national centralization and regional autonomy— the ancient and venerable city of Lisbon was being transformed into a cosmopolis of glass and steel. There was a measure of optimism all about; but like the roads far from the city, the visible transformation had the appearance of an overlayment that hid but did not alter an underlying terrain that generation upon generation had inherited and bequeathed. In my mid-twenties, before entering the University of Chicago, I was for several years a country musician, on the road. (Fortunately, no pictures remain.) I discovered onstage what I later understood more clearly from reading Plato's *Republic* in graduate school, namely, that any philosopher-doctor who intends to understand his student-patients would do well to attend to the sort of music that animates them. In Portugal, the musical genre that I kept being told to scrupulously avoid was fado, which roughly translated means "fate" or "lament." What, I wondered, was to be made of Lisbon's overt architectural transformation if the younger generation was so attentive to the chord of fate and lamentation that its members went to such great lengths to distance themselves from it?

Notwithstanding their protestation, the perdurance of the musical genre of fado confirmed a deep unease that my students in Lisbon felt about the gradual improvements wrought by commerce. Their dubiety could not be attributed to the melancholy of decline, however, as I had concluded was the case with my students in Buenos Aires. Something made the two groups similar, notwithstanding the differing economic trajectories. Neither economic decline nor advancement seemed to matter: my students in Buenos Aires and in Lisbon both seemed to be holding out against "commercial man" and the delinked, isolated condition he presupposed and portended, although I did not know why. I left Portugal that spring aware that what I had witnessed the previous two years in Argentina needed to be rethought. When I arrived in Buenos Aires five months later, I resumed the liturgical rhythm of my days and nights with palpable anticipation of an insight that never arrived, like a prayer that returns unanswered yet at whose silent center is an intimation of guidance yet to come.

September 11, 2001

I recall the long flight home from Buenos Aires to Washington, DC, in late August 2002 as being one tinged with sadness but not regret. Upon my return, I was to become the chairman of the Department of Government for the next three years—a large and encompassing task that I knew would preclude me from returning to Buenos Aires for the foreseeable future. Georgetown's government department is a remarkable place, not least because it takes self-governance seriously. When I first arrived in the mid-1990s, I was impatient with its procedures and conventions, its never-ending meetings, and above all its federal structure. By the time I was elected chairman, I realized that this immense and inefficient apparatus attenuated political cleavages within the department and helped assure that generational succession—always a delicate matter—went smoothly. Organize government so that long and necessary conversations between the various parties reveal the weaknesses of any grand plan, and you create a political body that proceeds less because a course of action is good than because the alternatives are worse. The politics of compromise are never grand. They are, however, durable.

It is true, but incomplete, to say that I became chairman because I was more or less next in line in the generational succession of faculty members who were deeply involved in departmental affairs. September 11, 2001, was the other reason. I have already relayed the conversation I had with my eldest son on the day before his generation found its formative event. During the fall semester of 2001, I had been granted a long-overdue sabbatical, most of which I had intended to spend either dockside or sailing on the Chesapeake Bay with Sabae (my half–black Lab, half–border collie) and with my laptop. The semester just under way, I settled in for a productive few months of writing, gently encouraged by the rhythm of the waves that my sailboat *Isabella*'s berth did not fully obstruct as they made their way in from the bay. Just one quick trip back into Washington to take care of some outstanding business and I would be set.

It was not a quick trip. Nor did my autumn of solitary writing turn out as I had thought it would. Had I not run an errand on my way into Georgetown to collect some books that fateful morning, I would have been on course to witness American Airlines Flight 77 detonate into the side of the Pentagon, instantly extinguishing the lives of 125 Pentagon personal on the ground and 64 souls in the air—one of whom was a Georgetown colleague and mother who had unsuspectingly boarded a flight with her husband and two young daughters that morning at Dulles Airport. On their way to Australia for the school year, their long flight ended abruptly less than an hour later. Lives destroyed without mercy—along with the lives of 2,751 others in New York City and 44 in a field just outside of Shanksville that agonizing morning. The rest of the day was spent trying to reach loved ones on jammed mobile phone lines and offering what comfort we could, never far from video footage of the Twin Towers exploding into flames and collapsing—at first with fine-grained scenes that captured fathers and mothers, sons and daughters, leaping to their death to avoid being burned alive by the inferno beneath their feet. No sooner were these scenes recognized for what they were than they were removed from view. Degraded as our public culture at times may be, we still have the good sense to recognize that there is no plausible commentary to accompany intimate scenes of orchestrated mass killing.

Some events are so hideous that even the passage of time does not render them comprehensible. Man, alone among creatures, inflicts evil and denies that he does so. Those inclined toward the view of the goodness and innocence of man called September 11, 2001, a "tragedy." The term was used loosely, of course, and was only partly a proxy for what the ancient Greeks had in mind. In tragedy so understood, there is no fault, only fated misunderstandings that yield affliction and sorrow as they unfold before us. There is, in short, no malicious will, no heart so horribly darkened that we are left breathless and mute, unable to comprehend what we witness. Tragedy is not evil; it remains on the scale of human foibles. There are no demonic proportions to it.

The tragic view of September 11, 2001, was that it might have been otherwise, that it was an anomaly, an exception that with the right foreign and domestic policy need not have happened, and need never happen again. In short, it could have been avoided with a little tweaking here or there. The tragic view of September 11, 2001, gives us room to bargain with events. America: a nation of traders.

When we are confronted by evil, on the other hand, there is no bargaining, no fine-tuning that changes the game. Our response to evil, thence, must be both greater and lesser than our response to tragedy: greater, because we are called to do all in our power to protect our neighbor; lesser, because our course of action must be governed by humility and prayer. As the weeks wore on after the attack, a clearer picture emerged of the enemy that America was facing. I tried to be attentive to these developments but was lost in despair over the brokenness of man. Huddled aboard *Isabella* for much of the rest of the fall as the Chesapeake Bay got rougher and the nights got longer, nature seemed not only unable to offer respite from evil, but seemed the very agent of it. Storms that would otherwise have been exhilarating now reminded me of how quickly the world could be undone. The clanging of the halyards against the masts throughout the marina turned into funeral bells. Such was my frame of mind. After receiving word that another Georgetown colleague, this one a friend in the government department, had perished in a Paris hotel just before Thanksgiving with his wife and young son, I was unreachable. Had the door of their hotel room not locked behind them as they stepped into the hallway to investigate the smell of fire in the air, they would likely be alive today. They died of smoke inhalation huddled together there in the corridor. More senseless death—which brought me roundabout again to September 11 and to the question of evil that it raised.

When we try to understand evil, we soon discover that we are not transparent with respect to ourselves. Such is the lot of a creature created in such a way that he can freely turn toward the darkness that he seeks to understand. That is our height and our unfathomable depth. No less than the man who denies the existence of evil, the man who seeks to comprehend it soon discovers that nothing is more certain than the vanity of our search for perspicuity about who we are. From Adam to the present day, man has been a problem to himself, an enigma he cannot outthink.

It was not duty alone, then, that brought me to consider becoming chairman of the government department; it was the realization that the proper response to evil involved neither intellectual vanity nor despair, but something of an entirely different order. More compelling than the call to duty was the dawning realization and dim hope that through the "sweat of my brow," a darkened world still benumbed by death and sorrow might somehow be made new, even if never fully comprehensible. Pascal wrote that distraction animates much of what we do. I did not seek distraction; I sought renewal—and threw myself into anything and everything that might abet that cause. What solace I might find would not come *to* my mind, but rather *through* my hands. I would help in the rebuilding of the world in whatever modest way I could, in the hope that even if understanding might not be possible, at some distant moment, measured more by toil than by the passage of time, regeneration would be.

Thinking back now, on that dark year of incredulity, confusion, and despair between September 11, 2001, and the time I became chairman the following September, I realize that it never really occurred to me that the missing pieces of the puzzle for which I had been searching while teaching Tocqueville in Buenos Aires the two previous summers might be found somewhere in the Middle East. The idea just seemed too implausible. September 11, 2001, had brought me to ponder evil and my response to it, but it had not yet entered my professional world, as an event to be understood in light of the story of the history of political thought that I knew so well. This is all the more surprising in hindsight because my Lisbon lectures and my last foray to Buenos Aires occurred after September 11, 2001. What had happened on that day could never have been far from my mind. I was intellectually preoccupied, however, with the newfound linkage between Lisbon and Buenos Aires, not with how what I had learned in those places might either shed light on September 11, 2001, or be illuminated by it. That thought never occurred to me. At any rate, upon becoming chairman, any progress I might have made in thinking along those lines was quickly halted by the administrative demands that daily came my way. I settled into the business of running a fine, even if highly complex, department. Three more years would have to pass before any further progress could be made.

From the Eastern Shore to Doha

I will forgo the details of my tenure as department chairman but give some evidence of the lengths to which I was driven in search of relief from its unrelenting pace by noting that in early February 2005, as I approached the end of my first term, I awoke in the middle of the night, reached for my laptop, and, as if guided by an invisible hand, searched for land on the Eastern Shore. The city of Washington may be the hub of American democracy, but it is a city set up for lawyers and doctors. The rest of us ordinary citizens, no matter how hard we work, always have to struggle there. I had had enough. After an hour or so of searching, I came across a description of a piece of property that beckoned. When morning finally arrived, I called the real estate agent. Within a few hours, I was trampling across three and a half acres of frozen wetland forest near the Chesapeake Bay, half certain that this was the place I would build a home and spend the rest of my years, and half certain that I had gone mad. The property and a house would be more than I could afford on my Georgetown salary. Not only that, it was a two-hour drive to Washington; how could I possibly come to work five days a week and live on the Eastern Shore? There I stood, underdressed for the winter cold as only a man who has spent too much time in the city can be, shivering in the beautiful silence of a loblolly pine forest, wondering how all the facts could line up against buying this little piece of paradise—and at the same time wondering why I was so certain that moving to the Eastern Shore was the right thing to do. A gentle wind blew through the pines, bringing with it the faint scent of bayberry. I turned to the real estate agent and said, "I'll take it."

We cannot know in advance how the course of our life is to change; at rare moments, however, we are presented with seemingly implausible choices that portend what is to come. A great deal hangs on whether we have the faith to take the first preparatory steps, even if they seem to lead into darkness. Such was the nature of my decision to move to the Eastern Shore. A moderate man would never have done what I did; but a moderate man does not live in anticipation and in faith that his world is a promise yet to be fulfilled, the significance of which he cannot now fully know. Six weeks later in a meeting back at Georgetown, I was embroiled in a pitched battle with one of the deans from the School of Foreign Service, defending the scope and purview of the government department's program offerings. Halfway through, in an effort to calm things down a bit, a recess was called. Out in the hall, my adversary turned to me and said, "Georgetown has just committed itself to establishing its School of Foreign Service in Doha, Qatar; I have been asked to be the dean, and I would like you to be on the start-up team. What do you think?" Without a moment's hesitation, I accepted his invitation. We shook hands like gentlemen, walked back into the meeting together, and resumed our battle. The contour of the immediate future suddenly seemed clearer, the decision I had made on that frozen February morning, less incredulous. Washington would remain the center of my life, but now in a new way. My home would be on the Eastern Shore; yet I would teach for Georgetown University in Doha, Qatar, half a world away, on the sunscorched Arabian Peninsula.

As I flew into Doha on an August night in 2005, I gazed at the yellow glow of the illuminated city below and could not help but remember the nightglow of the pyramids that teary night I had left Cairo more than two decades earlier. As the plane descended and the city below found its proportions less through my imagination than by the witness of my senses, I was suddenly overwhelmed by a feeling of repose, as if all the disparate and confusing facts of life were, for a moment, harmonious aspects of a larger whole.

During the month or so before the start of the school year, our meager but hardworking crew seemed more like a lost tribe wandering in the desert than a group of buttoned-down professionals ready to build a Georgetown annex on the shores of the Persian Gulf. The entire enterprise was hilariously incongruous at times: on the lush grounds of the main campus, the procedures and protocols of university life were second nature; now suddenly disoriented by heat, sun, and wind, even simple tasks confounded us. We raced forward to prepare for the start of classes, but our movement was akin to a dream in which you run but make no progress—here set against the backdrop of a shimmering ocean of sand.

The Age of Nations Has Not Passed

The day before our convocation, I learned that my niece and goddaughter—twin daughter of my twin sister—had put my name on the program to sing "The Star-Spangled Banner," without musical accompaniment, it turned out, though with other voices behind me. A recently graduated Georgetown Arabic major, she, too, had found her way onto the start-up team in Doha, in Student Affairs—and thought she would play a little joke on her dear uncle. Standing next to the dean, who informed me that he would sing loudly and quite off-key, the emir of Qatar not more than twenty feet in front of us in the first row, the words to our national anthem rang out of my mouth and his, and out of the mouths of the rest of the pilgrim souls up there on the stage. There was a moment of self-consciousness—we all felt it. Then palpable pride; it was undeniable.

As I sang on, fighting off a musician's impulse to harmonize with the dean, and attentive to that archaic feeling of pride that national membership brings, I thought about the quotation from Teilhard de Chardin inscribed above one of the auditoriums back on the main campus:

> The Age of Nations is past.
> It remains for us now, if we do not wish to perish,
> to set aside the ancient prejudices,
> and build the earth.

There on the convocation stage, however, the age of nations had not passed. This was not some supra-national project, but rather one involving that admixture of interest and generosity that has been the hallmark of most of what America has done in the postwar period. For the Qataris, that admixture obtained as well: the development of a superlative system of higher education would not only allow them soon to contribute to the worldwide conversation in the arts and the sciences, but also help develop thoughtful citizens capable of contributing wealth to their own nation.

The cosmopolitans among us would have it that nations are parochial and anachronistic. They can be, to be sure. But I fear there is no workable alternative to them in the foreseeable future. The impulse to form, maintain, and defend nations is too strong; and we would witness far more brutality in attempting to eradicate them than we do now from what they themselves commit. Perhaps, then, we are better served in this age of nations if we rise to the difficult task of greeting each other under the banner of hospitality. As hosts, we are called to welcome the neighbor who is not our own kind into our home, with a meal and an outstretched hand; as guests, we are called to show gratitude for what is offered and honor the conventions of the host's table. It is morally effortless to declare an end to the age of nations; doing so absolves us of the painfully difficult task of living in a broken and fractious world while still clinging to hope. Singing our national anthem at Georgetown's convocation in Qatar put to rest any lingering doubt that we were anything other than guests—of gracious hosts, I would add. We were Americans, in Qatar.

Teaching Tocqueville

Several days later, the school year began. One half of the two dozen self-conscious but friendly students in my class were Qataris, crisply attired in thawbs and abayas; the other half, dressed in conventional Western teenage attire, had homes elsewhere in the Middle East or Asia and, in one case, in the United States. All but three, I recall, were Muslim. Many were wealthy. Some were poor. I note these demographics because in what follows I discuss the opinions and understandings that my students voiced or intimated. They ranged widely, and no one view or set of views should be attributed to my Qatari students alone. Georgetown's new School of Foreign Service may have been in Qatar, but its students came from many nations.

If I had any grave apprehensions about the books I had chosen to teach, I do not recall them now. The seminal works of Plato, Augustine, Hobbes, Smith, Rousseau, Kant, Tocqueville, Marx, and Nietzsche are difficult to teach even on the main campus, in part because college students there are almost tone-deaf to the religious or anti-religious underpinnings of so much of what these authors wrote. While my students in Qatar were disadvantaged by not having had the thorough exposure to European and American history that my main campus students did, this deficiency was more than overcome by their tacit understanding that religion pervades much if not all of what we do and think.

These significant counterbalancing differences aside, both my main campus students and my students in Qatar suffered alike from shortened attention spans. In America, in Qatar, and around the globe, that is perhaps the single greatest threat to the future of higher education. A generation enticed and distracted by near-constant text messaging will find it difficult to understand that ideas worthy of the name are to be found in larger, more comprehensive amalgams like paragraphs, essays, chapters, and entire books.

Because my course on the history of Western political thought proceeds chronologically, the fall semester was well under way before I introduced Tocqueville's *Democracy in America* to the class. With the other authors I teach, I generally offer a few remarks about the ideas in the books we are about to study, and then focus immediately on what the author wrote, with a view of further elaborating my original remarks and to introducing additional ideas that can only be understood with patience and a willingness to suspend disbelief. Teaching Tocqueville over the years has taught me that my contextual observations must be much more extensive—not because what he wrote is distant and foreign, but, on the contrary, because it is so familiar. The things closest to us are always most difficult to see. Tocqueville's *Democracy in America*, I tell my students, is only indirectly about America of the 1830s; its real subject is the "distinct kind of humanity" that would appear in the coming age of equality—a kind of humanity increasingly delinked, isolated, and alone. As such, his book teaches all of us what we are already in the process of becoming.

I tell them, too, that Tocqueville was writing for a European audience. More precisely, he was writing for a European audience increasingly frightened by the emergence of this new, delinked condition and prone to respond to it by forming two parties, united by their fear and disgust of this new enemy, opposed by their assessment of how it might be destroyed. One party, the party of re-enchantment, sought to re-create an imagined past that never really existed; the other party, the party of revolution, sought to hasten the advent of a future in which all the heteronomies of the present moment have been overcome, and all lingering memories of the past obliterated. Why did these two parties—which appeal either to an innocent unity we can never recover or to justice in the world of time we can never achieve—emerge with such great force in Europe, he wondered.

In his wanderings through America, Tocqueville sought an answer to just this question. He soon discovered that while the Americans were further along on this trajectory of de-linkage and loneliness, the European impulse to re-enchant the world or to revolutionize it was largely absent. No small portion of *Democracy in America* is dedicated to exploring why that was so.

The Legacy of Anti-Modern Europe

As I began describing the outline of Tocqueville's account and began responding less to student argumentation than to something deeper, something more akin to resistance and incredulity than to argument, I heard myself saying things that were dimly familiar, though at first I could not place them. Then, suddenly, a flash of recognition: my students in Qatar were exhibiting the same palpable disbelief I had encountered years before in Argentina and in Portugal—not, strictly speaking, about America, but about the delinked modern condition itself, for which America was the evident proxy. How, I wondered, was this possible? My mind raced. The thoughts expressed by a majority of my students in Qatar were not simply similar to those of my students in Argentina and Portugal—they were identical: neither language nor history nor religion nor level of development made any difference. We are told that in ancient times a tower was built in Babel in order that man might ascend to Heaven. God punished the aspirants by destroying the tower and rendering nations thereafter incomprehensible to one another. That incomprehension certainly obtained in the case of the languages that the students in my classrooms on three different continents spoke. With respect to the ideas they understood and expounded, however, there was universal accord: delinked modern man was an error, a distortion, a ghastly mistake, and a frightful prospect. In regard to their thinking about delinked modern man, the Tower of Babel still stood. My students on three different continents spoke the same anti-modern language fluently.

What made this possible? Part of the answer came from the pages of *Democracy in America* itself. I have already mentioned the "distinct kind of humanity" that Tocqueville thought was beginning to emerge—namely, the delinked man I have nominally introduced already and whom Tocqueville occasionally calls "democratic man." That sort of man emerges amidst the ruins, however, of another distinct kind of humanity, namely, "aristocratic man"—the man whose life is constituted by his firm linkages to family, to land, to kingdom or empire, and, ultimately, to the cosmos itself. Pre-modern Europe was characterized by such linkages. So were Latin America and the entire Middle East. Indeed, the entire world was—or largely still is. America, alone, was and is the exception, a fact that helps explain why Americans are generally oblivious to the apprehensions that grip much of the rest of the world. My students in Argentina, Portugal, and Qatar were apprehensive and anxious about delinked modern man because they all came from societies where aristocratic linkages still prevail or are deeply etched into memory. Juxtaposed to the firm linkages they either still experience or remember, delinked man is, in part, a source of terror for them.

A common "aristocratic" history may explain why my students on three different continents had a generalized apprehension of delinked man. It does not, however, help us understand why the specific categories of thought through which that apprehension was expressed did not differ among them. A few comments about the intellectual and colonial history of Europe help explain the remarkable unanimity.

It is well to remember, first, that European thinkers had wildly differing assessments of the coming of the modern delinked condition. Tocqueville sought to identify its benefits while cautioning against its dangers. His was a sober defense of the coming age, which makes him the most important guide we have for the current troubled century: Tocqueville for a terrible age. There were notable anti-modern thinkers as well, however, whose response to the coming of modern delinked man was, as I mentioned, hostile through and through.

Second, the ideas of these later anti-modern thinkers did not simply remain quarantined in Europe. European colonialists either brought the ideas to colonial lands or brought thinkers from those lands back to Europe, where they were exposed to anti-modern ideas and then returned home, armed with thoughts that served as a template for further reflection on their own indigenous traditions of thought.

This has set the stage for the crises of the twenty-first century. In the twentieth century, European anti-modern ideas nearly brought an end to Europe itself; in the twenty-first century, the simmering theater for those anti-modern ideas is shaping up to be the former colonial lands of the Middle

East, although not only there. Perhaps the most remarkable thing about the various critiques offered of "the West" today, no matter where they appear in the world and no matter how different they appear to be, is that with a little probing their rudiments all can be traced to European anti-modern thinkers—notably to Rousseau, who dreamed of a re-enchanted world; to Marx, who saw in "capitalism" alienation, exploitation, and a war between those who have and those who have not; to Nietzsche, who saw in delinked commercial man a sign of the weariness and exhaustion of Europe; and to Heidegger, whose luminous thinking about Western civilization's "closure to Being" too easily invited a cult of death and recklessness toward the world that man had created through his proposing and planning.

The Battle on Three Continents

In Lisbon and in the rest of Europe, of course, no one dares suggest a return to the dangerous political experiments that nearly destroyed the continent during the last century—experiments in one way or another linked to the ideas of the figures I have mentioned above. The suspicion throughout Europe about delinked commercial man, however, has diminished very little and plays out daily in a tightly regulated economy and in ritualized politics that seem designed more to order life than to expose it to the uncertainties of liberty. The memory of the twentieth century stops the mind from wandering too far toward re-enchantment or revolution, but it does not stop it from wandering altogether. The ambition afforded to man extends as far as critique, but not as far as action. Denied the satisfaction of the deed, the postmodern movement had to have been born there.

In Buenos Aires and in much of the rest of Latin America, European anti-modern ideas continue to resonate as well, in part because European colonialists accomplished in Latin America something that never fully took hold in America to the north, namely, the development of a feudal system of landed property, sanctioned again by the Roman Catholic Church, as it had been in Europe, which passed property down in an unbroken chain from father to son. Here, occasional efforts to move toward less regulated markets, toward commercial man, are often seen as a means by which those who already have great wealth secure even more. Market commerce does a society good only if the chain of wealth between father and son is weakened, if not altogether broken, so that all men, no matter what their station, rise or fall from one generation to the next largely on their own merits, rather than because of their family pedigree. That has not yet taken place in Latin America. Little wonder, then, that anti-modern critiques of private property there often seem synonymous with justice itself, or that an Evangelical Protestant awakening has gripped Latin America, in reaction to a Roman Catholic Church whose alliance with landed property holders has sometimes trumped and sometimes been subservient to its allegiance to the poor. Oh, the multiple meanings of charity. Unable entirely to throw off the vestiges of a feudal past, and lacking the arrangements that might make the development of delinked commercial man more profitable for all, it should not be surprising that European anti-modern thought offers such solace on a continent that Tocqueville thought would see endless revolution but little real reform.

In Doha and in much of the rest of the Middle East, delinked commercial man does not yet exist. This is not to say that wealth, avarice, and greed do not exist. They do, just like everywhere else. It is important to note, however, that the way wealth is generated in the Middle East has little to do with the arrangements of commerce as Tocqueville and most Americans understand them. In America, commerce is inconceivable, for example, without delinked man freely moving about in search of the best price for his labor—hence the common term "labor market." Not so in much of the Middle East. There, states are largely patronage networks; corporations are generally cross-border joint ventures through which prominent families receive tribute from foreign companies intent on entering local markets; and rather than a free market for labor, workers are contracted through elaborate sponsorship schemes, which tend to the overpayment for much-needed American and European expatriate expertise, and to the gross underpayment of laborers and servants from other former colonial lands. My students in Qatar are familiar with these arrangements. Some of them even benefit from them. All of them, I think, wonder whether those arrangements can or will be maintained. Most of my students, for example, say they want "modernization" but not "Westernization." The latter is a catchphrase that subsumes, in polite form, the criticisms leveled by the European anti-modern thinkers who were introduced to the Middle East through colonial conquest. The former term, "modernization," is meant to suggest an alternative path, still unspecified, by which the improvements that commerce brings may be secured without the delinkage, perceived or real, that historically has accompanied such improvements in Europe and in America. Thus, "modernization" purports to be a path to prosperity that allows many if not all of the current social arrangements to remain intact. I doubt that is going to be able to happen. To some extent in Doha, and to a much greater extent in much of the rest of the Middle East, anti-modern European thought still fills the imagination of peoples neither quite able to embrace nor repudiate the world that is now upon them.

The Deeper Private Battle

Such is the public battle, there to be talked about, on three different continents. It would be incomplete, however, to leave off there. There is a deeper private battle occurring as well, which to the observer with eyes to see it only shows signs of intensifying. I have said that for my students around the globe, delinked modern man is perceived as a threat, and that there is remarkable unanimity about the nature of that threat. That is true. Indeed, without a way to voluntarily relink him, there will be no end to our troubles, for individuals, for nations, or for mankind as a whole.

The matter is made even more complicated, however, because this threat is simultaneously an alluring promise of release from the bondage of the predicates that constitute my students as sons and daughters, as cousins, as members of this or that tribe, or as members of this or that nation, even as adherents to this or that religion. In North and South America and in Europe, this alluring promise already visibly animates politics. The Middle East, by contrast, has been largely immune from these developments. Yet underneath the surface of the social, economic, and political arrangements in the Middle East that seem resistant to any effort to transform them, this gradual and irrepressible release amounts to a silent revolution whose consequences cannot yet be fully anticipated, even if they can be already felt. The Tahrir Square uprising in Cairo, about which much has been made, is but the first skirmish.

Tocqueville saw this radically new fact of human history to which my students in the Middle East and elsewhere bear witness. He was, in fact, among the first to understand the ambivalence that "democratic man" would feel toward his emerging condition. I think it is safe to say that my students from the Middle East experience this ambivalence far more so than do my students in North and South America or in Europe. A heated argument in class one day brought me to propose that if my students thought so little of delinked man, then I would collect all of their mobile phones and return them at the end of the semester. We all laughed, but the point had been made: around the world, the mobile phone has facilitated a level of independence that previous generations could not have imagined and given an advantage to young men and women in the age-old battle with their fathers and mothers over how much influence tradition and inheritance will have. My students in Qatar were quick to offer criticisms of delinked man, but in their own lives, in what they palpably affirm, they show ample evidence that they are rushing headlong into the very condition they claim to deplore. Repulsed and drawn to it in the same instant, my students in Qatar, and to no small degree everywhere else in the world, live with an agonizing contradiction they cannot resolve, no matter how many text messages they send.

By and large, my students in Qatar are still far less delinked than many of my students on the main campus at Georgetown. And in many ways that is salutary. In the course of our class discussion that semester and beyond, however, I began to realize that the fateful question was not how delinked this or that group of students happened to be, but rather whether they could conceive of an alternative to the fatal temptations of either re-enchantment or revolution that seem to be invited by the modern delinked condition itself.

That is, I believe, the momentous political question of the twenty-first century, not only in the Middle East but everywhere. This is why Tocqueville is so important. My years at Georgetown's main campus, my forays to Buenos Aires and Lisbon, and my several years in Doha have convinced me that the next generation is ill-equipped to conceive of a salutary alternative to these temptations. In how they think of themselves, in how they think of the generation of wealth (commerce) and the regeneration of society (family), and in how they think about religion, they typically recur either to dreamy ideas about a past that cannot be retrieved or to revolutionary ideas that dispense with the whole of their inherited history. Worse still, they sometimes alternate between both. The seriousness of the problem has become all the more clear each year I have taught Tocqueville. More than a great book, *Democracy in America* is a Rorschach test that reveals the reader's apprehensions about the delinked condition in which we all find ourselves. I came to Doha without fully understanding what teaching Tocqueville in Arabia would reveal. I left convinced that vigilance, for citizens of every nation, must involve stepping back from the precipice toward which the ideas of both re-enchantment and revolution fatally draw us; and that we must all keep our eyes forever fixed on the painful fact that the delinked, vulnerable, and exposed condition in which we find ourselves in the modern world can be ameliorated but never cured—least of all by political means.

We are in sore need today of understanding just what sort of amelioration is actually possible in modern life. In the Middle East, the conceptual apparatus for this understanding does not yet exist, I fear. In America, I think it safe to say that our habits still point us in the right direction, even if our thinking increasingly leads us astray. When delinked citizens withdraw into themselves, their imaginations invariably wander toward "isms"—capitalism, corporatism, socialism, communism, environmentalism, feminism, postmodernism, multiculturalism et al.—that promise to put an end to the void in their lonely souls but cannot. Hovering over the world, but no longer in it because they are distracted rather than engaged, delinked citizens dream of a perfect world, free from the stain and corruption that our neighbor perennially reminds us is the lot of man, and whose face brings an abrupt end to our dreamy imaginings. When citizens only look upward to the visible power of the state, when the neighbor is lost from view, is it any wonder that our national politics becomes a battleground where one fleeting dream of perfection is set against another, and that somnambulant, self-absorbed citizens increasingly die alone, with cats?

The Question Before Us

Herein lays the remaining great challenge to our generation and to the next. As I think back on my conversation over coffee shortly after I arrived in Doha in the fall of 2005, and remember my café companion telling me about how he and his generation responded to their fathers, I am reminded of the revolution that Tocqueville announced: the breaking of the bonds that held generations together, one to the next. We have not reached the end of that historical drama. Nor can we know, in advance, what the end of that drama will bring. If Tocqueville is to be our guide, there are two great alternatives before us. The first involves an imperfect liberty requiring strength of soul, neighborliness, and an understanding that perfection is not the lot of man. The second involves a despotic form of equality still without a name, in which docile and delinked citizens look upward to the powerful state rather than outward toward their neighbors for their nourishment. They will be entertained, but not happy; free to think as they wish, but seldom listened to; publicly empathetic, but privately resentful; unencumbered by grinding obligations, but wracked by the apprehension that their lives are but an anonymous dream.

I recoil at the thought of this second alternative, but wonder whether we are already too sleepy to be awakened; or whether we still have the fortitude to labor, by the sweat of our brow, to secure that imperfect liberty that is ours.

2 *Man, the Lonely Animal*

Breaking the Links

In a letter composed just three years before his death, Tocqueville wrote: "This profound saying could be applied especially to me: it is not good for man to be alone."[1] When I tell my students that the whole of *Democracy in America* was written under the aegis of this sentiment, under the shadow of what could be called a philosophy of loneliness, they listen. Tocqueville's concern, I tell them, was the emergence of a new type: *homo solus*, the lonely man; and with how this new type would understand himself and his place in the world. And so my students approach Tocqueville's *Democracy in America* with a sense of urgency. They soon discover that it is a book that reads their own hearts, for few things are more haunting to them than the specter of loneliness. They seek to understand Tocqueville, so that they may understand themselves; for in Tocqueville's writing, they find an account of the etiology of the disease from which they suffer. Man, the lonely animal. That is why I ask my students around the globe to read his book. And because teachers of the history of political thought are called not only to diagnose disease but to indicate wherein health may lay, I ask my students to read *Democracy in America* so that they may also discover Tocqueville's cautious hope that such loneliness need not be the final word about their future.

While loneliness has been chronicled in all ages, Tocqueville thought that it would be an especially acute problem in the democratic age, because the antidote that the aristocratic age before it had offered would no longer be available. That antidote was the "links," as he called them, which tied each to everyone else. In his words:

> Aristocracy has made of all citizens a long chain that went up from the peasant to the king; democracy breaks the chain and sets each link apart.... [Democracy] constantly leads [each man] back towards himself alone and threatens finally to confine him wholly to the solitude of his own heart.[2]

The character of these links is not easily understood in the democratic age, which explains why they cannot be easily reconstructed. In the democratic age, man is largely gathered together by having interests in common. In the aristocratic age, man is largely bound together through loyalty and obligation. Interest involves conscious, ongoing calculation and negotiation between *individuals* who gather together and then disband; loyalty and obligation entail range-bound and durable relations between *roles*.

It is difficult for my main campus students to imagine the ties of loyalty and obligation. I routinely ask them, for example, whether what they do at home in the way of "chores" is undertaken because the family into which they have been born requires it. The description already anticipates the answer. Very few raise their hands. The formulation itself seems odd to them. More than any generation that has come before, they expect and receive money for the chores they do and are seldom moved to action without it. When they are young, they are called upon to attend various family gatherings and do so; but from adolescence onward, it is increasingly difficult to concentrate their attention on such matters. Already they are on their way to breaking their attachment with their parents. Loyalty and obligation can hardly be fortified if sons and daughters begin to leave the family fold shortly after they reach puberty. And because the lesson of self-interest has often been instilled long before that, it only seems natural that it should be extended and amplified when their eyes shift elsewhere. To this should be added Tocqueville's concern that as the administrative reach of the state extends itself further and further into everyday concerns, the real sway of the family is bound to diminish. When sons and daughters anticipate that the state will keep their affairs in order from cradle to grave, they soon come to think of it as the real source of their sustenance and reproduction. That, too, encourages them to think largely in terms of their immediate interests. Nothing can really dissuade democratic man from thinking narrowly about himself if the state has taken away from him the cumbersome task of living with his family and his neighbors.

My students in Qatar, on the other hand, tell a different story. They are ever cognizant of the family name they bear and of both the loyalty that must be displayed and the obligations that must be borne. These do not diminish with age. Many of them, especially the women, spend evenings and weekends involved in family celebrations that routinely include first and second cousins. These gatherings bring coherence to the extended family and reconfirm its standing within the larger body social. This attentiveness to family obligations often has deleterious consequences for their studies, though in vain does the teacher implore them to place their own self-interest at the forefront. Many do not understand themselves first and foremost as individuals but rather as bearers of a family name. More accurately, while they are increasingly coming to think of themselves as individuals, they nevertheless continue to understand themselves as occupying a specific and largely unalterable role in their families and, by extension, in their societies. They occupy *roles*, yet they think of themselves increasingly as *individuals*. Therein lays their difficulty.

In America, Tocqueville thought that the state would tend to gradually undermine the family; that is why he wrote that all our efforts should be directed at fortifying the family. In parts of the Middle East, on the other hand, the extended family has become further entrenched by the development of a strong state, since it is largely through a state patronage net-work that families receive their bounty. Thus, in parts of the Middle East, my students are pulled both toward the delinked condition that characterizes the democratic age and toward the roles they occupy as members of this or that family. This tension cannot increase forever without consequence.

To think of oneself as an individual rather than to under-stand oneself as a role is really a rather remarkable historical achievement, which my main campus students largely take for granted. The Latin term *persona* supposes a distinction be-tween the actor and the mask he puts on. In the aristocratic age, the mask—the role—largely mediates relations. The in-dividual behind the mask may strain to find the right way to wear it, but it cannot ever be wholly removed. In the demo-cratic age, when everything is on the move, the mask seems ill-fitting and has the appearance of an awkward artifice. If donned at all, it is seldom worn for long. It is often in-tentionally removed and sometimes stripped off by oth-ers. In bemused moments, it is treated ironically; when it appears grotesque to its wearer, a caricature of the beauty and purity of the individual behind the mask, the tender and never-ending search for "authenticity" commences. The in-dividual, alone and without durable linkages to others of the sort that roles can provide, searches for "meaning" in a world that seems inhospitable to his "needs."

When permanence in the social order is assured, then man can be at home in the role he occupies; when no such perma-nence exists, as is the case in the democratic age, man finds what permanence he may by thinking of himself as a disem-bodied individual who steps into the fray, hopefully at his own discretion, from some seemingly unmovable vantage point. My students in Qatar are not yet fully exposed to this fray. Their families, and the still largely fixed location of their families in society, provide them with a stability that for my students on the main campus is almost unimaginable. Both groups discover a measure of permanence, though they find it in different locations: the one in the roles they occupy in their families; the other by hovering over the world as individuals. That is why the language of "authenticity," so prevalent in America, is scarcely heard in the Middle East.

Decorum

There are implications for decorum that follow from the distinction between roles and individuals, which are worth mentioning. In the Middle East, students in class are usually quite cognizant of the standing of their families in relationship to others. In America, this is true to a much lesser extent, if at all. In some parts of the Middle East, for example, it is impossible to form a PTA because certain families will not condescend to talk to or even be seen with other families of lesser stature in the same room. That does not happen in America, though other tensions certainly exist. In the classroom, this familial stratification sometimes takes the form of one student deferring to another when a teacher poses a question. For an American disposed to believe, say, as Thomas Jefferson did, that an aristocracy of talent—a "natural aristocracy," as he called it in his 1813 letter to John Adams—was the only one that can finally be tolerated, this can be maddening to witness.

On the other hand, there is also something quite heartening about manners that are scripted in advance. Knowing that they speak not simply for themselves but for their families, when they disagree with their classmates, it is with the cognizance that their families are in some way intertwined outside of the classroom as well. This would never enter the minds of my students on the main campus. They are there to debate and dispute, which makes the character to their discussions sometimes harsh and abrupt. They do not know each other's families and speak only for themselves, at that moment, often with little concern for their relations, past, present, or future. Decorum is hard to maintain when only the present moment matters. My students in Qatar are no less prone to short attention spans than my students on the main campus; their lives have taught them, however, that they do not only speak for themselves, that they occupy a role in their families that mediates all that they say and do. For that reason, they are more circumspect in how they comport themselves in class.

The matter is made more complicated by the fact that underneath the brusque demeanor of my American students is a deep insecurity and sense of homelessness that stepping away from the family usually occasions. When their ideas are shown to be flimsy or without foundation, they become quite fragile and sometimes feel that they have been treated "insensitively." Their reason is not yet fully formed, and so they rely on their personal feelings as a guide and compass. My students in Qatar are no further along in the development of their reason; they are, however, accustomed to the lesson of shame that extended family loyalty invariably teaches. Guilt may animate the individual, but shame is necessary if family name plays a large part in the ordering of the larger community. Thus, where my students in America are at once brusque and fragile, my students in Qatar are decorous but also accustomed to enduring what for American students would be brutal humiliation. This admixture of decorum and brutality among my students in the Middle East is not something my American students much understand; on the other hand, the admixture of abruptness and fragility among my American students is something quite perplexing to my students from the Middle East.

Living in the Moment

I have suggested that to think of oneself as a disembodied individual, as my American students largely do, is also to think almost without regard to the past or the future. When the past, present, and future are connected in a long and unbroken chain, Tocqueville tells us, the father is the natural link that holds the different moments together. When the father loses his position, as he does in the democratic age, the time horizon of each successive generation begins to collapse into an instantaneous "now." I ask my American students if they can imagine acting with a view to what their grandparents and their unborn grandchildren might think about their public and private deeds. They cannot; they are, figuratively speaking, fatherless children. My youngest son, I tell them, routinely asks why our own house should be filled with furniture that my father and mother inherited. When I tell him that it is not mine to dispense with—that it belongs not to me, or to him or his older brother, but to his grandparents and his grandchildren— he rolls his eyes in disbelief. My students on the main campus are amused by this story, but most of them hold to their opinion that they should continue living in the moment. What can their family name mean under these circumstances? How can they understand what role they play in the succession of generations when the sentiments and thoughts that matter are largely those that happen to coalesce spontaneously?

My students in Qatar, on the other hand, can easily imagine acting with a view to what their grandparents and grandchildren think. Not surprisingly, their fathers generally play a more prominent role in their lives than do the fathers in the lives of my students on the main campus, especially when it comes to marriage. In the way they dress, comport themselves, and speak, they sense themselves being watched over by generations past and future. This is one of the reasons that American life appears alien to so many in the Middle East. Proceeding, as Americans often do, as if only the moment matters is almost inconceivable for them. When music videos made their way to the Middle East, there was the foreseeable objection that the insinuated sexual content was *haram*, forbidden. But more telling was the incredulity that the video scenes themselves lacked a context that might give them coherence, let alone significance. They were perceived to be no more than dreamy and gratuitous imaginings that flitted from one provocation to the next without a plot. The sexual impropriety of these scenes was clearly at issue; but the more revealing objection pertained to the scope and motivation of the action that was portrayed. What sort of men and women are these, who act on impulse, and whose lives dance from one disconnected event to the next? They were certainly not men and women from the Middle East, the guidance for whose movements is choreographed by the whispering community of generations that their roles prepare for them to hear, even before they are born.

The Framework of Infinite Possibility

It would be misleading to say that my students in Qatar are guided in their actions solely by the roles that extended family lineage bestows. I have noted that they understand themselves as occupying roles but that they increasingly think of themselves as disembodied individuals. In class one day, I wondered aloud how far along this development had proceeded. Most of them indicated that they saw the significance of their roles diminishing and their status as individuals to be the most significant thing about them. They are young, of course, and cannot fully know how marriage and the burden of raising sons and daughters will temper their current thinking and return them to roles to which youth has already familiarized them. Still, it is telling that they can—and do—increasingly think of themselves as disembodied individuals who, like many of my American students, hover over the world rather than being engaged in it. They are living, as Tocqueville put it, in "an intermediate age, a glorious and troubled period in which conditions are not fixed enough for the intellect to sleep."[3]

Most of my American students, as I have said, think of themselves almost entirely as disembodied individuals and seldom, if at all, as occupying a role. They, too, will learn in due course that they are burdened by the precarious task of generation, and that this task cannot be successfully undertaken without condescending from the heights they now think they inhabit. From that distance, all things seem possible; and the role, say, of father or mother is one they can scarcely imagine—or, rather, they imagine that no real bounds need be set on the kinds of fathers or mothers they will be. That is why they enter into marriage so ill-equipped for what invariably follows. My students in Qatar, on the other hand, may occasionally lose sight of the roles they occupy, but because they still largely believe that marriage is a matter of unification of families more than of personal choice, they are somewhat more prepared for what follows. That is changing, however. Divorce rates are on the rise throughout the Middle East—with all that this implies about the breakdown of durable roles and the emergence of the disembodied individuals that Tocqueville predicted would occur in the democratic age.

While my students in Qatar wrestle with what it means to be located in an intermediate stage between occupying a role and thinking of themselves as individuals, my students on the main campus wrestle with how life might be lived without roles altogether. Rather than occupying an intermediate age, they look back from the far end of the development that Tocqueville thought would take place in the democratic age, and cannot help but think that roles are limits on their person, which ought to be opposed whenever they are encountered. They do not commence their thinking from the standpoint of limitation and occasionally ponder a breach, as my students in Qatar do; rather they begin from the framework of infinite possibility and think of roles altogether as a constraint. Tocqueville had warned of this new impulse that now prevails amongst my students on the main campus.

> As castes disappear, as classes get closer to each other, as men are mixed tumultuously, and their usages, customs, and laws vary, as new facts come up, as new truths are brought to light, as old opinions disappear and others take their place, the image of an ideal and always fugitive perfection is presented to the human mind.[4]

One of the awkward discoveries that students from the main campus make when they come to Qatar for visits or for junior year abroad is that many of the students they meet there do not think of themselves as "oppressed" by the roles they occupy. To be sure, there are things about their societies that they would like to change, but on the whole they seem no less uncomfortable with their societies than my main campus students are with their own. From within the framework of infinite possibility, this comfort appears to be a form of false consciousness, from which my students in Qatar should be "liberated." It is not. From within the framework of infinite possibility, *all* roles, *all* less-than-cosmopolitan understandings, are a form of false consciousness. Re-education, therapy (if the problem runs deeper), and war (if the problem can only be dislodged through destruction) are its correctives. My students in Qatar alternate between being annoyed and being amused by these predictable encounters, which invariably reinforce the view already prevalent in the Middle East that for all their high-minded talk, Americans really believe in nothing at all. Little wonder so many in the Middle East think that American ideas are corrosive or vacuous. As a consequence, they do not want the "liberation" that democratic man offers. And they do not want it because they cannot imagine living in a world that presupposes infinite possibilities.

Ease of Social Relations, Natural Affection, and Sympathy

Before I further explore the inner workings and implications of this frame of mind about which Tocqueville so worried, some things must be said about what is gained when democratic man comes to think of himself as a disembodied individual. Loneliness may be the obvious drawback to life in the democratic age, but the de-linkage that fosters a sense of loneliness also alters the terms of engagement with others, sometimes in salutary ways. When my students on the main campus greet me these days, they will often say, "Hey, Professor Mitchell." I am sure they see me wince. I am old enough to remember a time when students could not have conceived of addressing their professor in that way. My students in Qatar occasionally greet me in an informal fashion, but the practice has not yet really caught on. I suspect it is done at all because they hear American students speak that way. I cannot imagine that they address adults from their own society in a similar manner. This ease and informality of relations is one of the hallmarks of the democratic age. If Tocqueville is right, we can expect more of it in the future, not only in America but around the globe.

To be at ease in social relations entails a deep familiarity with the protocols and conventions that each role requires— or it entails the absence of roles altogether. My students on the main campus increasingly live as if the latter were true. They often think of formalities as archaisms; and in their speech, comportment, and dress, they make no distinction between lounging around at home, going to the shopping mall, showing up for class, or attending church. Not occupying a role, they have nothing to demonstrate or to prove. They are largely content "just being themselves," in whatever setting they find themselves.

The unwillingness and inability to make distinctions invites a certain coarseness of manners—mobile phone maletiquette, public slovenliness, and other indelicacies not worth mentioning. Nevertheless, what attends these poor showings is a straightforwardness and honesty that derives from always needing to get right to the point. It is not out of disrespect that this straightforwardness emerges. On the contrary, it emerges because of the belief in the democratic age that, together with his neighbors, man is engaged in a grand and forward-looking enterprise of building a world that he can clearly imagine though not yet see. True though it is that he too often settles into the moment and wishes to stay there forever, when rousted from his indolence, he worries that the future world he envisions will slip away before he can grasp it, and understands that he must speak simply and without subterfuge to others if he is to be successful. Knowing he must count on his neighbor, he must give every indication that he can be trusted by him. Unable to hold fast to any role that would assure his standing in perpetuity, he must forever reach out to his neighbor with an outstretched hand and with goodwill in his heart. While this does not eliminate his poor manners, it certainly attenuates them—if not throughout his day, at least for some portion of it.

The unruliness of American society is one of the first things that my students from the Middle East notice. They wonder how the Americans can accomplish anything at all under these circumstances, let alone be great. The answer is that without intact and unchanging roles on which to rely, democratic man must reach out in trust to his neighbor and speak without subterfuge, or else give up and withdraw into himself altogether. Without the aid of durable roles, through which he could look with reverence to the past for guidance, unruly democratic man must look forward to a future that he cannot build alone. An ease in social relations can make such a future possible.

In addition to the ease of social relations that the democratic age makes possible, natural bonds of affection, to compress Tocqueville's usage,[5] emerge—really for the first time in history. This is quite an astonishing claim, which bears investigating. In the aristocratic age, where relations are mediated through the roles that are occupied, the thought that natural affection should prevail and direct the course of action scarcely enters the mind. Any dim impulse of affection that emerges soon dissipates if its object is not within grasp. Unnourished and unable to make its demand felt, it is soon extinguished.

When the social world begins to be disrupted and roles no longer fully mediate relations, desires that were once quickly extinguished enter the mind and remain there, enlivened by the prospect that the social arrangements that precluded their satisfaction will soon be removed. In Europe, this intermediate stage was the age of romanticism. Here the heart soars at one moment, only to be dashed at the next. In democratic America, there was no equivalent, because the roles that proscribed natural affection were never as pronounced as they had been in aristocratic Europe. As Tocqueville put the matter:

> For whatever the credulity of passions may be, there is scarcely a means by which a woman may be persuaded that you love her when you are perfectly free to marry her and do not do it.[6]

Romance in America, such as it is, has always had a practical cast to it; the ease of social relations brings honesty and candor; but the social equality that brings about such ease also curtails the imagination, makes it generally dull, and sometimes crass. Seldom does it soar; rarely is it sophisticated.

My students on the main campus take for granted that natural affection should prevail in their own relations. In their friendships and in their romantic life, it scarcely occurs to them that they should arrest an affection that their heart declares. Publicly they are reluctant to admit that natural affection should be constrained in any way and generally feel embarrassed when conventions or prejudices make themselves heard in spite all their efforts to blot them out. This will change as they get older, although they certainly deny it; the conventions and prejudices of their fathers and mothers will reemerge, though in a more attenuated form than has been the case for previous generations. That is inevitable as conditions become more equal.

My students in Qatar, on the other hand, are still largely guided by the roles they occupy and so cannot imagine that natural affection should wholly guide them in their affairs. Their friendships are arranged more carefully, as they must be in a society that is ordered by the logic of familial standing rather than by individual choice. They are, in fact, quite astonished by how freely the American students they meet allow their hearts to wander.

In this still-aristocratic condition, it would be tempting to think, as Tocqueville did, that the heart exacts its revenge through romantic intrigue when natural affection is largely ruled out; and that relations between men and women in America are therefore healthier than they are in the Middle East. In some respects, I am sure that is true, though there is reason to worry that the more my American students think of themselves as disembodied individuals, the more misguided and reckless their relations become. I return to this matter in another place. This important caveat aside, natural affection is one of the more important achievements of the democratic age. When roles diminish and conventions lose their hold, man is almost forced to listen to his own heart. What is heard is seldom coherent and often contradictory. That is why my American students struggle so and take so much longer to grow up than do my students from the Middle East. When natural affection is the guide, a thousand errors will be made; and from the vantage point of a society with intact roles, the entire enterprise will seem a grand folly. That judgment might be justified if, in fact, the breakdown of roles that accompanies the emergence of the democratic age could be stopped or reversed. It cannot; and I suspect that as generation succeeds generation in the Middle East, each will find itself increasingly confounded by the tension between what roles require and what natural affection declares.

Aside from an ease in social relations and natural affection, the third great achievement in the democratic age is sympathy. When a vast and unbridgeable chasm separates families, classes, tribes, or castes, no real sympathy is possible. Then, obligation and loyalty hold the entire social edifice together, and true sympathy is unknown. Only when social barriers begin to fall does the man who once seemed different in kind now appear to be different only in degree, if at all. Then his sufferings become recognizable, haunt the imagination, and serve as a wellspring of political action.

Almost all of my students on the main campus are haunted by the suffering of others and think that the sole purpose of social policy or political action is to eliminate it. When I tell them that Tocqueville thought that the sympathy they feel can only fully emerge in the democratic age, and that throughout history disregard for the suffering of others has been the rule rather than the exception, they are surprised. When their gaze fixes on a nation in which a family, class, tribe, or caste is inured to the suffering of others, they are apt to wonder how such an arrangement can be borne; yet it does not occur to them that there can be no sympathy without a notion of a common humanity in which each man participates, quite irrespective of the predicates that attach to him. In the aristocratic age, where each family, class, tribe, or caste is a species of humanity unto itself, replete with its own internal codes of honor, the idea of a common humanity scarcely enters the mind; and so sympathy is largely absent.

In Qatar, my students are perplexed by this fixation American students have about eliminating suffering on a global scale. It is not that they have no concern for others. Indeed, Islam, like Christianity and Judaism, is clear about the need to take care of widows, those who are poor, and those who are otherwise in need. My students from the Middle East are disposed to support the Red Crescent, which, like the Red Cross, does relief work in a spirit that verges on being religious without being explicitly so. Yet they cannot quite escape the suspicion that something more than religious charity is at work in the minds of the American students they meet, something that is only thinkable when man is no longer really a member of a particular family, class, tribe, or caste. Severed from any real social location, most of my American students are capable of sympathy for people elsewhere in the world they will never meet, but too frequently do not even know their neighbor next door. In the Middle East, on the contrary, generalized sympathy of this kind scarcely exists, though well-articulated and concrete obligations and loyalties do.

Disposed as he was to think that health always lies between nodal extremes to which man is naturally drawn, Tocqueville, on the one hand, applauded the development of sympathy in the democratic age: suffering would thereby be cast in a brighter and broader light, and the prospect for a truly kinder and gentler world would emerge. On the other hand, his endorsement of sympathy was tempered by the worry that attentiveness to the suffering of others far away would come at the cost of reduced concern for the neighbor next door. God's love may be Infinite, but man's is not: concern and solicitude perennially directed over the horizon diminishes what is available for the neighbor who stands in front of you.

Emblematic of this emergent sentiment about the distant suffering of others is the upsurge of humanitarian assistance in all of its forms, which is unthinkable for peoples whose allegiance still aligns with their family, class, tribe, or caste. Not surprisingly, American foreign policy has been increasingly guided by just this sentiment, much to the dismay of political realists, who argue that foreign policy should be concerned with identifiable and discrete national interests. In the Middle East, where the generic suffering of others has not yet captivated the imagination, there is a strong suspicion that American foreign policy in the region cannot really be about what it declares—for what nation would sacrifice blood and treasure to alleviate the suffering of others far beyond its borders? Surely there must be another, more sinister, motivation.

Yet for Americans, the thought that humanitarian assistance should guide foreign policy slips naturally into the imagination. I suspect that the curricular changes that have occurred in our colleges and universities during the past generation are both a cause and a consequence of this discovery of universal sympathy. Not long ago, the burden of education involved a disciplined exposure to literature, history, mathematics, science, and the practical arts through which the next generation became thoughtful citizens of a middle-class commercial nation. Today, increasingly, education has become an occasion, if not a pretext, to nurture the sentiment of universal sympathy that only disembodied man can fully believe—hence the deliberate attempt in our public schools to undermine national pride and any other discrete affiliation, and the platitudes that make this effort innocuous: "sharing and caring," "everyone is special," et cetera. This development, long in the making, has now configured public debate so that our presumption is that America *should* offer humanitarian assistance nearly everywhere, and that for such assistance not to be extended, strong arguments to the contrary must be provided.

However sensible and compassionate this policy may seem to democratic man, its effect will be to draw America into foreign entanglements the intricacies of which we cannot fathom, and inflame the suspicions of our enemies and our allies alike. "Helping" sometimes doesn't.

Sympathy extends man's moral universe; above all, sympathy overrules his temptation to yield to self-satisfaction. It rousts man to reflection, if not to action. To dream of infinitely extending sympathy to the point where democratic man takes the suffering of the whole world in upon himself, however, is to imagine powers that he simply does not have. Many of my American students do not yet understand this; they go too far in their sympathy and, in doing so, lose sight of their neighbor—or, rather, precisely because they are always losing sight of their neighbor, their sympathy goes too far. Very few of my Middle Eastern students, on the other hand, dream of infinitely extending sympathy. Like students nearly everywhere else in the world, they live through the roles they have inherited and easily understand the obligations and loyalties they have to those around, above, and below them. While they often long to see further, they still strain to do so.

The picture I have given thus far of my American students is that they are easygoing, oriented by natural affection, and prone to sympathy. Tocqueville thought that these dispositions would make life in the democratic age not only decent and honest, but also warm and considerate. Improperly understood, they can also bring about the pathologies I have briefly identified above. This picture of my American students is incomplete, however, without some consideration being given to their relationship to money.

Money

I mentioned earlier that my students on the main campus cannot imagine doing their chores because the family into which they have been born requires it. They do their chores not because of obligation and loyalty, but because of the money they receive. The softer dispositions just considered might seem to be at odds with this incessant expectation that money will come their way for all that they do, but Tocqueville thought that the increased focus on money—like the ease of social relations, natural affection, and sympathy—was inevitable in the democratic age. As he put the matter: "In aristocratic nations money is the key to the satisfaction of but few of the vast arrays of possible desires; in democracies it is the key to them all."[7]

Why does money become so important in the democratic age? When loyalty and obligation are the real bonds that hold society together, as they are in the aristocratic age, work done or services performed do not always proceed with a view to payment. The "payment," in fact, sometimes does not involve money at all, but rather the discharge of an obligation. Here, money is sometimes out of place; if offered or requested, it might even cause offense. In such a society, there are, so to speak, several economies: the larger and less palpable economy whose currency is loyalty and obligation; and the smaller and more measurable economy whose currency is money.

In the democratic age, obligation and loyalty diminish in importance. As roles are abandoned, loyalty and obligation become less and less thinkable. Each man increasingly thinks of himself as being alone, as an individual who hovers over the world but who is never quite bound to it. As this self-understanding grows, the vocabulary of individual choice and self-interest comes to predominate, and thoughts of money fill the imagination. Cut off from others and alone, without deliberate effort, democratic man can expect nothing of his neighbor, and his neighbor can expect nothing of him. The less palpable currency of loyalty and obligation almost disappears, and money becomes the chief means by which the business of society is undertaken. In the *Manifesto of the Communist Party*, written in 1848, Karl Marx put the matter in the following way:

> The bourgeoisie, wherever it has got the upper hand, has put an end to all feudal, patriarchal, idyllic relations. It has pitilessly torn asunder the motley feudal ties between man and man than naked self-interest, than callous "cash payment."[8]

Tocqueville saw the same development but did not think that "capitalism" brought about this near obsession with money. Rather, he thought that money became the universal currency, so to speak, for the same reason that the ease of social relations, natural affection, and sympathy emerge so prominently—namely, the growing conditions of social equality, which undermines the economy of obligation and loyalty.

My students in Qatar are quite baffled by this constellation of American attributes and wonder how they hold together at all. The image of the greedy, money-loving American, of Marx's heartless bourgeois man, is often fixed in their mind. That there is more to the Americans than just that attribute generally comes as a shock. Perhaps the most common thing Middle Eastern students say when they visit America for the first time is that they cannot believe how *nice* Americans are. Marx could never have predicted this.

For money to become the ubiquitous measure, the "feudal, patriarchal, idyllic relations" found in the aristocratic age must have more or less succumbed to the conditions of social equality about which Tocqueville wrote, and man must have found himself delinked and alone in a seemingly contingent world. My students on the main campus often tell me that they think of themselves in this way. Yet when pressed to think about their future and about how this necessary focus on money bears on the question of how they will have a family or live in the surrounding natural world that makes both wealth and family possible, they pause with some discomfort, then rehearse an answer that generally echoes the answers given a generation ago when their fathers and mothers wrestled with the same questions.

When they think about having a family, they often argue that financial considerations—whether their career is intact, whether their house is big enough, whether they have a large-enough savings account—should take precedence. When they think about the surrounding natural world, they often argue that financial considerations—can profit be made at the expense of pristine nature?—should be ruled out entirely. The general sentiment is that any clear-thinking student will understand that family must be understood in light of financial calculations, and that nature, on the contrary, must not be.

The female students I teach will face the issue of family most directly. On the main campus especially, they are delinked enough to believe it important to find high-paying careers, for they alone are responsible for their destiny. Yet they also know that it is through them that civilization will reproduce itself. And so they are torn. "What is the value of motherhood," many of them ask, "when money is the only value?" It is relatively easy for them to see that before the advent of the democratic age, money was not the only value. They nevertheless largely prefer the current arrangement. They recognize that the fundamental task of reproduction can never be banished, but also that the unbounded opportunities that are now theirs go hand in hand, with money becoming the ubiquitous measure. The value of "motherhood" must therefore run headlong into the ever-growing value of money. This is a dilemma of the democratic age that can be awkwardly balanced, but I do not think it can be resolved.

In Qatar, the dilemma is less apparent, for now. Family, in its extended form, plays a much larger part of the women's lives there. And so at first glance, the value of money has not yet made its assault on the value of motherhood. This is not quite the case, however. A college degree in America has been long recognized as a way for men and women to advance their careers and to earn more money. In the Middle East, a hybrid version of this understanding has developed: there, a college degree is increasingly a way to "marry up" into a family with higher social—and therefore economic—standing. A college degree is still the path to more money, but it is *through* the family, rather than in spite of it, that the increase often occurs. In America, the domain of the family is in conflict with the ubiquitous value of money; in large parts of the Middle East, that is not yet the case. Someday soon, I suspect it will be.

Environmentalism and Stewardship

All of my students wrestle with the question of how the value of the natural world can be understood in light of the ubiquitous value of money. What I say here largely pertains to my students on the main campus. I mentioned a moment ago that my main campus students believe that the pristine natural world cannot be assigned a monetary value. Nature, they claim, must be cordoned off from the world measured by money. Many of my students would call themselves "environmentalists." Ansel Adams posters hang on their dorm room walls, as they did for my generation—and through their beauty declare that money is not the only measure of value. In general, my American students think of nature as pristine, benign, and innocent. Their use of the term "environment" as a proxy for the natural world indicates that man is not always already *in* nature but rather than he can be separated from it—thus the familiar locution "man and his environment." Many of my students think this way because they have been raised in urban or suburban settings. Wishing to locate innocence somewhere, but not finding it in man, they locate it in nature, which is distant enough from them so as not to be able to disabuse them of their fancy.

Students who have been raised in exurbia or on a farm or in a fishing village could never think this way: they know that man is always already in nature. Consequently, they tend to think in terms of stewardship rather than in terms of "environmentalism" and are not apt to see a stark opposition between the value of nature and the ubiquitous value of money.

Money must be spent in order to elicit from nature her full glory, and nature must be appropriated to make money. Under the banner of stewardship, both tasks will always be in tension but always be necessary.

Under the banner of environmentalism, however, the rapprochement between nature and money has either taken the form of cordoning off nature entirely from the activities of man or of the buying and selling of pollution credits, which purport to put a moneyed price on the damage man does through his activity. The environmental community is happy with the former, while large and successful industrial enterprises — for reasons I explain in the next chapter — are happy with the latter. Faced with such formidable and entrenched opponents, whose opposition is only apparent, the call to stewardship, like a lost voice crying out in the wilderness, can scarcely be heard. I will address a weary supposition underlying environmentalism at the end of the next chapter. Here I can only intimate that stewardship, which presumes that man does not hover over the world but is always already in it, offers a hopeful alternative.

The Changing Face of Authority: Soliloquy and Public Opinion

In the previous sections, I began by talking about the delinked condition in the democratic age and the loneliness it brings.

I paused to consider how that condition alters the terms of engagement with others, sometimes in salutary ways. In the democratic age, the ease of social relations, natural affection, and sympathy emerge almost spontaneously. This confuses many of my Middle Eastern students. They cannot make sense of what they see because while they can easily understand that the delinked social condition leads to loneliness, their own social condition is not nearly as equalized as the one in America is. The salutary benefits of social equality therefore scarcely exist. They are also somewhat put off by the extent to which money rules the hearts of the American students they meet; yet their affection, too, grows for it, in spite of their protestations.

These considerations are important, in part because of what they reveal about the differences between my students on the main campus and my students in Qatar. There is, however, a more significant development that occurs in the democratic age, which both groups of students evince in almost the same measure. It is troubling that they each increasingly comprehend their worlds in this similar way. Tocqueville knew this would occur, worried about it, and thought that efforts must be undertaken to counteract it.

This development about which Tocqueville worried was an almost inevitable consequence of the breakdown of the aristocratic age. When each man is linked directly to the next and has only dim ideas about a generalized humanity, truth does not float freely above the nexus of social relations but rather tends to be mediated through them. An idea is believed or disbelieved more because of the standing of the man who says it. In the democratic age, on the contrary, man's tutelage is generally limited to the early years of childhood, after which point he comes to believe that the authority of others has little or no bearing on the truth he is able to discover. He trusts himself alone, as Tocqueville put it, "and claims to judge the world from there."[9]

I have already noted that my students on the main campus are more disposed to think of themselves as alone and on their own than are my students in Qatar. The ties of family are looser among them, and from an early age they have been taught that the purpose of the education they receive within and without the family is to prepare them to leave the family. My students in Qatar, on the other hand, are still largely bound to their families in ways that my students on the main campus cannot understand. Nevertheless, when I ask both groups of students if they think the truth of an idea is linked to the authority of the person who propounds it, of one accord they tell me that they alone must make that determination. My students in Qatar may still be attentive to the place of their family within the larger society, but they *also* increasingly believe, like my students on the main campus, that the only verifiable locus of authority lies within. Increasingly like them, they "claim to judge the world" without reference to an authority outside themselves. My students in Qatar are pulled, therefore, in two very different directions. My students on the main campus have little understanding of how agonizing that can be.

When the locus of authority shifts from others to the self, as it must in the democratic age, there are no doubt great benefits. Man is almost forced to think for himself, and if all goes well, he emerges from his silent acquiescence to those above him and speaks publicly with an authorial voice. There is another possible consequence of this shift in the locus of authority, however, that is not so salutary: the delinked condition that all but invites him to disengage from active participation in the world may tempt him to withdraw entirely into himself. There, seemingly self-satisfied and alone, his encounter with the world, such as it is, takes the form of soliloquy rather than active engagement.

Almost all of my students are ensnared by this temptation and show little interest in escaping from it. Indeed, many of them cannot imagine that their encounter with the world *could* take any other form than the presentation of the soliloquy they have carefully crafted, for themselves and for others. Under the guise of "social media," they post a representation of themselves to "friends" they seldom see or have never met, which has little to do with the actual life they live. They also often mark their day by virtual events that transpire around their home page. While they may bring their computers to class, the ideas their teachers attempt to convey are often not enough to entice them away from the singularly important task of crafting themselves online. In their outreach to their "friends," they live within themselves. In the midst of this apparent abundance, I cannot help but think that this is evidence that when man has been spared from the always awkward face-to-face relationships through which society is nourished and reproduced, his life becomes impoverished, and, in spite of his protestations, he is most truly alone.

This collapse into soliloquy, which so many of my students begrudgingly confess, is only one aspect of the shift in the nature of authority in the democratic age. Tocqueville pointed out that the destruction of the "authority of a name,"[10] as he called it, not only invites soliloquy and solipsism; it also elevates the standing of public opinion in ways that would have been inconceivable in the aristocratic age. When each man is delinked and alone, he may be proud of his independence, but he is also cognizant of his diminished stature, as well as the diminished stature of everyone else he sees. Looking up, he no longer sees any particular man hovering over him to whom he must be ever attentive. Rather, the singular entity that is always in his sight and on his mind is "the public," which speaks to him in the form of public opinion.

Tocqueville was not alone, of course, in understanding the growing power of public opinion in the democratic age. Writing about his native America in 1838, James Fennimore Cooper remarked in *The American Democrat*: " 'They say,' is the monarch of this country.... No one asks '*who* says it,' so long as it is believed that '*they* say it.' "[11] Tocqueville, however, seemed to understand that both soliloquy and "they say" *together* would

constitute the new way in which authority would be understood in the democratic age. The "authority of a name" in the
aristocratic age would give way to the bifurcated authority
my students witness in the democratic age: on the one hand,
authority is vested in an increasingly disengaged self; on the
other hand, authority is vested in public opinion.

Both my students on the main campus and my students
in Qatar, as I have said, understand one portion of the bifurcated authority found in the democratic age. Many of them
live largely in and through their soliloquies. Interestingly, my
students in Qatar are not yet as attentive to the public opinion
portion of authority. In the Middle East, family standing still
matters. So long as this is true, the first things that my students
there see are the families around them, not "the public," which
does not yet palpably exist. My students in the Middle East
are, it is true, cognizant of what could be called global public
opinion. In that sense, they live bifurcated lives akin to the sort
many of my students on the main campus do. They watch the
same movies and television shows, know the same songs, and
are attentive to the same passing fashions, even if they cloak
it under the attire that convention demands. In addition, they
well know how to converse in the global discourse of "rights"
and "freedoms."

In many of their own countries, however, there is no further
evidence of a broad sense of the public than this. When my students from the main campus visit the Middle East, one of the
first things they notice is the imposing compound walls that
surround so many of the houses and the garbage that is nearly
everywhere. Qatar, I should note, is remarkable for its clean-
liness, though compound walls are ubiquitous. Elsewhere,
however, American students wonder how it would be possible
to care for gardens that flourish inside compound walls and
yet ignore the garbage immediately outside the compound
gate. When societies are an amalgam of families, as they are in
the Middle East, the idea of a public in which each man participates quite independent of his familial location cannot easily

take hold. Each family jockeys for position with other families above and below it, but seldom sees any further.

It is often said that American society is too "individualistic" and that, as a consequence, it has no sense of the public. Nothing could be further from the truth. In the current age, it is in non-individualistic societies, where family looms large, that there is almost no sense of the public. The garbage outside the compound gates in many parts of the Middle East attests to this absence. So, too, does the so-called "Arab Street," which is better understood as a fierce apparition of a public space that cannot yet take form precisely because family name and political party have the authority that they do. From this can come conspiracy theories based on perceived or real humiliations—but not public opinion.

When social equality comes to prevail, each man thinks of himself as standing alone, it is true; but when he has lost his ties to his extended family, the public is bound to loom large. The open front porch of the single-family home, not the high compound wall of the extended-family network, is the concomitant of public life in the democratic age.

These caveats about the status of the public in the Middle East aside, it would seem that living in this bifurcated way would be quite difficult for my students, both there and on the main campus. The distance between these nodal points of human experience, between soliloquy and "they say," is vast; and it is hard to see what one could possibly have in common with the other. I ask my students this question, and in their self-searching moments, they tell me that as different as these nodal points are, what unites them is that they allow my students to maintain their distance from the messiness of human relations. They update their home page; they jot down and comment here or there for a "friend," spontaneously, of course; they all know and chatter about the latest television programs or games—and they fall asleep at night rehearsing their soliloquies to themselves, in a recurring loop that can be halted by the one thing many of them are most frightened to do, namely, involve themselves in actual face-to-face relations—not for a moment, but for an extended period. As Tocqueville put the matter: "Sentiments and ideas renew themselves, the heart is enlarged, and the human mind is developed only by the reciprocal action of men upon one another."[12]

My students are more "connected" than any generation in the history of the human race. They nevertheless sense themselves to be alone. The two nodal points of soliloquy and public opinion are where they live, so to speak. It is hard to overstate the danger that is harbored in this bifurcated existence that risks nothing. Tocqueville's defense of civic associations in particular and of federalism in general was meant to address it. I return to that defense at the end of this chapter. Next, however, more needs to be said about the education my students receive, with a view to exploring how it contributes to that danger and how it may be attenuated.

The Hermeneutic of Suspicion

The delinked condition of the democratic age not only facilitates the heightened sense of loneliness my students experience; it also establishes the sovereignty of the individual in all matters of deliberation. What hold can the authority of others have on their understanding once this has occurred?

In the aristocratic age, I tell my students, the situation was otherwise. In 1637 René Descartes wrote his now-famous *Discourse on Method*, in which he dares to suggest that for knowledge to be trusted, it must not be accounted as true if it rests on the foundation of custom or the authority of others. One of the philosophical harbingers to the democratic age, Tocqueville noted that the Americans are Cartesian without even having read Descartes. As he put it:

> To escape from the spirit of system, from the yoke of habit, from family maxims, from class opinions, and, up to a certain point, from national prejudices; to take tradition only

as information, and current facts only as useful study for doing things otherwise and better ...: these are the principle features that characterize what I shall call the philosophic method of the Americans.[13]

Most but not all of my students on the main campus intuitively adopt this democratic mode of understanding, if such a term can be used. They instinctively recoil at the notion that an idea should be taken seriously because of the authority of the name associated with it. Especially in America, the prevailing notion is that the political philosophers I have them read have no authority whatsoever over them. Doubtful, therefore, that there can be such a thing as a Western canon, they are reflexively disposed to approach the books we read with a hermeneutic of suspicion, as it has been called.

The term "hermeneutic of suspicion" is of postmodern origin, but in Tocqueville's idiom, it merely names a democratic prejudice about authority. Doubtful that anyone can really teach them anything they have not already discovered by their own lights, my students are ill-disposed to patiently entertain the finally unprovable wagers that all great philosophers make concerning the world, its wellsprings, and how we must, accordingly, live—unless and until my students become convinced that the questions those philosophers ask are already their own questions. Even then, the preeminent attitude is often doubt rather than deference. On more occasions than I can remember, I have looked into the eyes of my students as I have entered the room and recalled my father telling me of the nearly audible words his students would murmur as he walked into his Middle Eastern history classes at the University of Michigan in the 1960s: "I dare you to teach me anything."

There is something salutary about this hermeneutic of suspicion. It draws man out of the complacency that can easily befall him if he accepts an idea on authority alone. Moreover, because the democratic age summons each and every person to become his own arbiter in nearly all matters, it is inevitable that a hermeneutic of suspicion should have the place that it does in our educational institutions today. "Critical thinking" is everywhere, as it should be. At its best, this encourages the development of our faculties and contributes to the formation of that most precious and rare gift: an authorial voice.

The Hermeneutic of Deference

I do not think, however, that education worthy of the name can be achieved by the hermeneutic of suspicion alone. When suspicion is the singular principle of education, the result—unintended to be sure—is a collapse into solipsism that is no less debilitating than the complacency that blind reverence can produce. Education worthy of the name surely cannot involve a blanket dismissal of ideas because of where or when they emerged, or because of the particular people who have held them. Yet today that judgment has been definitively made by a vast number of students who have been nourished exclusively by the hermeneutic of suspicion. Convinced that they have found a reason to dismiss much of what has been written in the past, many of my students on the main campus think of their philosophy courses as they would a visit to a mausoleum. They wonder, in fact, why the books they read should have been declared monuments and placed there at all—and by whom and under what authority. They wish to live among the living, who they think can neither be indebted to nor overshadowed by the dead.

Their restlessness suggests otherwise. In the democratic age, each generation looks at its predecessor as an archaism and revels in the novelties it has discovered and by which it has been captivated. Man, however, can never find nourishment by feasting only on what the present moment has to offer. The more he tries, the more restless he becomes. "I should be surprised," Tocqueville wrote, "if mysticism did not soon make progress in a people uniquely preoccupied with its own well-being."[14] Sooner or later, evidence mounts that man's momentary impulses are flawed and his deepest convictions have been but opinions and prejudices on which no fully adequate life can be built.

My students on the main campus are restless but wish to believe that the popular culture on which they have been raised provides them with all that they need to build a successful and nourishing life. In Qatar, this restlessness is evident as well, though the problem is not yet as acute as it is on the main campus. In the 1960s, I tell them all, my generation, too, feasted on the crumbs that popular culture offered. College campuses, however, were ablaze with debates of which my students today can scarcely conceive. Freud (for whom man was sick), Marx (for whom man was alienated), and Smith (for whom man could trust his conscience and his assessment of his own interests) all seemed to be viable alternatives, over whose ideas titanic battles were fought. The mood was that of anticipation, of a future freed from illnesses of the mind and of the body social, in need of one last great push forward to get us there. The popular culture of the period, as debauched as it at times was, reflected that sentiment. The ironic, post-historical posture adopted by nearly all of my students today had not yet taken hold. In the 1960s, the struggle lay ahead; for many of my students today, irrespective of the *personal* struggles they endure, the social and historical struggle of ideas is largely over, and all that remains is to implement "social justice." Amidst this certainty, their restlessness nevertheless obtrudes. Only under providential circumstances can they be persuaded to listen.

It would be futile to declare to them that canonical texts should be read because through them the full depth and breadth of their civilizational legacy is revealed. In the democratic age, the claim that their forefathers can help them find their way is bound to be questioned. Besides, many of them doubt altogether that there is a hidden depth and breadth to be discovered. In the democratic age, therefore, education worthy of the name must start with an appeal to experience—more precisely, it must begin with the gentle intimation on the part of the teacher that the "hooks" on which students "hang" their experience are not numerous or well-placed enough for them to understand their lives. That is, the task must be to show that the hooks they have received from popular culture are not adequate for what they in fact already experience but cannot quite yet understand.

For this wager to be evaluated, the hermeneutic of suspicion, which they know by heart, must for a time be suspended. In its place must be enthroned a dangerous *maybe*—maybe the canonical authors can provide them with hooks on which to hang their experience; and that for those hooks to emerge into the light of day, students must, for lack of a better term, engage in a hermeneutic of deference. This takes the form of supposing for a moment that the canonical authors may, in fact, have understood a great deal more than my students accredit to them, and that the finally unprovable wagers found in their books are nevertheless worthy of my students' attention anyway. Plato noted in the *Republic* that about the most important matters, conclusions "are hard to accept, but also hard to reject."[15] Education involves more than the conveyance of information; the soul itself must be turned or reformed for there to be education properly understood. There is no explicit algorithm to bring this about. Neither suspicion nor blind reverence will cause it to happen. In the democratic age, suspicion prevails and reverence has all but disappeared. The task of the teacher, therefore, is to gently educe from students the recognition that they, too, have been feasting on crumbs.

When students begin to realize that they actually hunger, their disposition changes. Although they continue to trust in the authority of their own experience, they now solicit help from the authors they read so that they may understand it more deeply. In this sometimes agonizing condition, which a teacher may draw them toward but never resolve for them, real education—the turning or reforming of the soul—transpires, and a more ample basis for life is discovered.

I do not doubt that this type of education is a rare achievement. While I cannot prove it, I suspect, nevertheless, that such an education is more necessary for self-government than is often imagined. In the democratic age, man is too easily disposed toward solitude. He senses himself to be cut off and alone, and without a basis for communion with his neighbors, with nature, and even with himself. A hermeneutic of suspicion will always slip naturally into his thoughts. A hermeneutic of deference will invariably be an afterthought, so to speak, which takes hold only in the aftermath of the discovery that what he has been given in the way of his own opinions or the popular culture around him cannot satisfy his hunger. The hooks on which to hang experience are not exhausted by what the prevailing opinions of the current moment provide. That is the wager of every educator, and one of the most important tasks set for institutions of higher education in the democratic age.

Higher Certification and Other Hazards

I have suggested that most of my students are reluctant to adopt a hermeneutic of deference because they think they must "judge the world" for themselves. That is true. There is another reason as well:

> As men become more alike and the principle of equality penetrates more peacefully and more deeply into institutions and mores, the rules of advancement become more inflexible and advancement slower; the difficulty of quickly reaching a certain degree of greatness increases. By hatred of privilege and embarrassment over choosing, one comes to compel all men, whatever their stature might be, to pass through the same

filter, and one subjects them all indiscriminately to a multitude of little preliminary exercises in the midst of which their youth is lost and their imagination extinguished.[16]

These rather prescient remarks have been confirmed by developments in higher education over the last generation. Indeed, it is tempting to say that what occurs in our many of our colleges nowadays amounts less to higher education than to "higher certification," perhaps even "higher stupefaction." The amount of coursework required is often staggering and reflects political bargains struck among faculty constituencies rather than an overarching consensus about the kind of democratic citizens our colleges should aspire to graduate. It is not unusual for students to take five and even six courses a semester, many of them mind-numbing prerequisites that train them to flirt with ideas but not fall in love with them. Barely able to discuss an idea let alone write about one in depth or with coherence, the tests my students take are more and more geared to "measurable outcomes," to use current educational parlance, which overthrows an older if never fully realizing understanding of the labor that teachers are called to perform—namely, mentor and midwife. This relationship now almost fully undercut, if students are anxious, searching, and unsure of their bearings, they head over to an obscure corner of the campus for "counseling" rather than to their professor's office—where in the not-too-distant past, such "problems" might have been treated in light of the range of insights the canonical authors would have offered about them.

To these immense constraints in, and modifications of, college life should be added the proliferation of "service learning" and extracurricular activities, which further distract students from grappling with ideas in the classroom even while they fill out their résumés with yet another line item. Too hindered by never-ending requirements and too frightened that their résumé will be one line shorter than the student sitting next to them, there should be little wonder that students think of college in terms of certification rather than education, or that most of them graduate without having the good opinion of their suspicion tempered by a breathtaking encounter with a seminal idea that reconfigures their understanding of their own experience.

In the democratic age, college education comes to be thought of as a universal right. As more and more students are accommodated and "forced through the same filter," the bond between teacher and student must of necessity be weakened, and the art of reforming character through education nearly abandoned. In order to facilitate this new situation, the older classroom—which required only important books, desks, chairs, blackboards, professors, and students—is being replaced by an impoverished but immensely more expensive high-tech, virtual, online, and remote "learning environment," the cost of which is ultimately borne by mind-boggling student loan debt and federal funds that behold colleges to national government in unsavory ways as never before. This cannot end well.

There is a third, no less troubling, reason why my students are reluctant to adopt a hermeneutic of deference. During the last half century or so, there has been a tectonic shift in the way history has been taught. A perusal of the course offerings at most colleges will reveal scarcely a course about the singular actions of "great men" and many courses about social history—notably that based on "race," "class," and "gender." In the aristocratic age, the task of the historian was to provide exemplars for human conduct, as would be expected in an age when men looked to the past for models of action, commerce, beauty, and piety. In the democratic age, when each man becomes small and the body social looms large, a different kind of history gets written, as Tocqueville explained:

> In reading the historians of aristocratic ages and particularly those of antiquity, it seems that to become master of his fate and to govern those like him, a man has only to know how to

subdue himself. In running through the history written in our own time, one can say that man can do nothing either about himself or his surroundings. Historians of antiquity instruct on how to command; those of our day hardly teach anything other than how to obey. In their writings, the author often appears great, but humanity is always small.[17]

Tocqueville did not think it inappropriate to attend to social history; he did think, however, that overemphasizing it in the democratic age taught a dangerous moral lesson to students: namely, that no single man, armed with clarity of mind and formidable character, can alter the course of history. Habituated by the mode of history-telling that pays little attention to individual greatness, the very idea of adopting a hermeneutic of deference seems quite odd. My students on the main campus believe that the world is animated wholly by the social forces of race, class, and gender. How might an in-depth and patient study of a canonical author's ideas, which would require a hermeneutic of deference, possibly benefit them? The hermeneutic of suspicion that comes so naturally to their imaginations is in some measure a consequence of the necessary prejudice about social forces in the democratic age. It is therefore very difficult to counterbalance.

Higher Education in the Middle East

In Qatar and in many parts of the Middle East, the imbalance I have noted on the main campus and at other colleges across the United States does not yet exist. I dare say, in fact, that the hermeneutic of suspicion is still largely in its nascent form there. My students do not yet understand themselves to be disembodied individuals and so can only occasionally imagine what it might be like "to judge the world" without reference to an authority outside themselves. Nor has higher education become so universally available that students in the Middle

East are "forced through the same filter." In addition, the idea that history involves the movement of social forces rather than "great men" has not yet penetrated their imagination.

To these considerations, treated above, must be added another. Tocqueville wrote that whether a nation has had a political revolution or has cast aside its religion increases or diminishes the general level of suspicion toward the current state of things. Europe, of course, has both had political revolutions and largely cast off its religion, and so it is not surprising that the hermeneutic of suspicion figures so conspicuously there. In America, there was a political founding but no revolution. Religion here, moreover, has not quite been cast aside. That is why in America the hermeneutic of suspicion is not as prominent as it is in Europe. Said otherwise, European society is center-left, while American society—though not its colleges—is center-right. In parts of the Middle East, the political upheavals of the mid-twentieth century largely replaced an aristocracy based on family and land with an aristocracy based on party and political patronage. There was violent upheaval but not revolution—or, rather, there were largely unsuccessful revolutions. Religion, moreover, retains its central place, notwithstanding the changes that may be under way. For this reason, and for those mentioned above, the hermeneutic of suspicion has not advanced in the Middle East as it has elsewhere.

In light of what I have been arguing about the importance of the hermeneutic of deference, this would seem to suggest that in this one regard higher education in the Middle East is healthier than it is in America. That is not true. It is well to remember that higher education in the Middle East, with a few notable exceptions, was set up and organized when the British and French controlled the region. What remains are highly specialized, highly centralized, and governmentally controlled colleges where the deference is to the teacher—though not to canonical authors, who are generally not taught at all. To this should be added that the acquisition of knowledge is often measured by how well students memorize the material their teachers have presented and repeat it back to them verbatim.

Knowing that this model cannot produce thoughtful students or entrepreneurial citizens, there is a great push by government education ministries to reform higher education. What could be called a teacher-centered model is being replaced by the latest educational fashion to sweep across America: "student-centered learning." In America, fortunately, colleges have a long and venerable history, and only slowly do the latest fads from our educational experts make their way into the classroom. That is not the case in much of the Middle East today. Whatever else their governments and citizens may think of U.S. foreign policy in the region, ministries of education are eager, indeed fervent, that their institutions of higher education receive accreditation by U.S. accrediting agencies. By virtue of their very weakness, many of those institutions are therefore likely to be remade from the ground up, relying on techniques and theories that are dubious at best. Most notably, the prejudice that all teaching must have a "measurable outcome" now entrances and hobbles both administrators and teachers alike in the region. Georgetown's Qatar campus is fortunately immune from some of this nonsense, in large part because the curriculum run there is identical to that offered on the main campus. Elsewhere, however, the outlook is not so bright. When pressed to offer a vision of what their students should understand about their civilization and the world at large, teachers and administrators are reluctant to hazard a guess. The "advances in education" that our experts here in America are eager to implement everywhere therefore will probably be put to the test most completely in the Middle East and elsewhere in the developing world, where well-meaning ministries of higher education do not yet see the danger.

I have already conveyed my worries about my students on the main campus. The popular culture in which they are immersed cannot cure their restlessness or their solitude; and the hermeneutic of suspicion they bring to bear on their studies closes them off to the very ideas that could provide the feast for which they hunger. The worry I have for my students in the Middle East is greater still. They do not suffer from an almost genetic disposition to be suspicious of ideas that come their way based on "the authority of a name." Yet their institutions of higher education may soon be re-formed in such a way that what they most need—namely, an exposure to a liberal arts curriculum that draws them out of themselves—will not be provided; and this because such courses do not easily yield the measurable outcomes that forward-thinking ministries of higher education think must be demonstrated.

A Deeper Kind of Inquiry

Can a liberal arts education in the Middle East produce thoughtful citizens who are able to think both critically and deferentially? I cannot but think that the great challenges of the twenty-first century will require, among other things, that we "[seek] a refuge under a little wall from a storm of dust and hail driven by the wind," as Plato called it in *The Republic*.[18] The blur of daily events in the Middle East fogs the mind, and when an effort is made to withdraw into the citadel of thought to understand them, the terms of the analysis immediately at hand often oscillate between what can loosely be called nineteenth-century liberal triumphalism and twentieth-century post-colonial indignation. The one is unmindful of the intransigent fact that liberty is not the metanarrative of the Middle East; the other, professing to support the indigenous peoples there with a clean conscience, adopts *European* anti-modern tropes in order to defend them. In short, the analyses rely on ideas that emerge over the period of the two-century wound that is European colonialism but go no further. Even when purportedly pure Islamic thought is brought forth, it is, I venture to say, suffused with and over-whelmed by European anti-modern tropes. In sum, the terms of the debate are as one-sided as was colonialism itself.

Much more is needed. My discussions with administrators, teachers, fathers, and mothers in the Middle East have con-vinced me that while they know their institutions of higher education must be reformed, they are also frightened by the prospect that their sons and daughters, like ours in America, may very well acquire knowledge that can be "measured," but that such knowledge will contribute little to their understand-ing of the civilization that is their inheritance. So empowered, they will go through life adhering to, as Tocqueville wrote,

> incoherent opinions that are encountered here and there in society like those fragments of broken chains that one some-times sees still hanging from vaults of an old building, no lon-ger supporting anything ... [like] an unknown force [that seems] to carry [them] along towards a goal of which they themselves are ignorant.[19]

They will, in short, lack the reflectivity and fluency needed to grasp the wagers made by the canonical authors who formu-lated the range of understandings that constitute their own in-heritance and those of members of other civilizations.

We flatter ourselves to say that ours is the first global cen-tury. There is, nevertheless, an urgent need for us to begin a global conversation that neither starts from the pretense that there is a "universal human discourse" nor from a sup-position that reifies civilizations or groups within them into sacrosanct and impervious "identities." Beyond the blur of events, beyond the well-worked-out oppositions between lib-eral triumphalism and post-colonial indignation, lies a third alternative—still without a name, which might be called com-parative canonical inquiry—that seeks to return to the ori-gins of all durable civilizations and trace their development through the great ideas that are registered in their respective canons.

My students in the Middle East are right to ask me why I only teach the canonical authors from the West. I tell them that I have spent a lifetime trying to understand why and how those authors may be still important for us, and that I am able to take them that far but no further. I can, nevertheless, imagine a day when a generation of scholars with a deep and reverential knowledge of their own inheritance sets itself the noble goal of placing before students around the globe the great ideas that have shaped civilizations—not in the form of taste-testing survey courses, which make all such ideas seem unpalatable, but in the form of an extended feast, which demonstrates beyond a reasonable doubt why those ideas have nourished the minds and hearts of generation after generation. "Variety is disappearing from within the human species,"[20] Tocqueville wrote, with alarm. Commerce and trade can hasten that disappearance; memory and habit invariably fortify the variety that remains. I suspect that only something like comparative canonical inquiry can provide a foundation substantial enough for members of different civilizations to stand on and to engage in the kinds of conversations that will be required if we are to greet each other under the banner of hospitality during the rest of this already troubled century and beyond. In the Middle East in particular, a liberal arts curriculum that includes canonical authors from its several overlapping civilizations can move students beyond the borders of thought established by the historically provincial antinomies of liberal triumphalism and post-colonial thought. In the safety of this more ambitious classroom, students can find their way to ideas that they might finally call their own, through a communion with canonical authors who give them reason to believe that they must make a longer journey if they are to find a viable antidote to the solitary, delinked condition of the democratic age—one that takes them back much farther than the last two centuries. By virtue of the sentiments and habits that already vie for the right to rule in the minds of millions of Middle Eastern students—elicited as they have been by social media, mobile phones, and text messaging—liberal arts education of the capacious sort I have envisioned here is peculiarly well-suited for a generation in search of a voice it cannot yet find.

Loneliness and Political Polarization

Higher education can and should play a prominent role in attenuating the delinked condition my students in America already understand and my students in the Middle East at times fear. What I consider in the remaining pages of this chapter pertains not to higher education but to American politics. One of the questions that most perplexes my students in Qatar is why American politics is so polarized. Can this bald and painful fact about the American polity be understood, they wonder, in light of Tocqueville's claim that the democratic age is characterized by de-linkage and loneliness? At the heart of their question, I think, is wonderment about whether the American polity has become so wounded that it cannot recover. I remind them that Tocqueville thought that the strength of the American polity arose not from individual men acting alone, nor from governmental administration acting on behalf of them, but from the face-to-face relations that are nourished when politics is decentralized and the spirit of liberty prevails. Earlier, I cited a passage from Tocqueville that bears repeating here: "Sentiments and ideas renew themselves, the heart is enlarged, and the human mind is developed only by the reciprocal action of men upon one another."[21]

The principal wager of *Democracy in America*, contained in this passage, is that face-to-face relations are sorely needed if democratic freedom is to endure. They are needed largely because democratic man is delinked and alone. Through the associations he forms with his neighbors, he is drawn out of himself, his world expands, his faculties are engaged, and his disposition is enlivened. This is the inner secret of democratic freedom and the basis of Tocqueville's worry about the growing administrative power of the state.

> Democracy does not give the most skillful government to the people, but it does what the most skillful government is often powerless to create; it spreads a restive activity through the whole social body, a superabundant force, an energy that never exists without it, and which, however little circumstances may be favorable, can bring forth marvels. Those are its true advantages.[22]

And elsewhere:

> Administrative centralization, it is true, succeeds in uniting at a given period and in a certain place all the disposable strength of the nation, but it is harmful to the reproduction of strength. It makes [a nation] triumph on the day of combat and diminishes its power in the long term. I can contribute admirably to the passing greatness of one man, not to the lasting prosperity of a people.[23]

These compelling endorsements of limited government have not, I think, been understood in their proper light. Commerce, a contemporary argument would have it, benefits when the national government is limited. That is probably true—but that is not what most concerned Tocqueville. He thought that as democratic man became more and more delinked, he needed to be *voluntarily* relinked. A strong national government, even one that is eminently fair and efficient, cannot do that. Only face-to-face relations can.

When face-to-face relations abate, a number of things happen. I indicated in the first chapter that Tocqueville thought that democratic man was untethered man, in desperate need of salutary bondage, so as to protect him from himself; and that one of the consequences of living without such bondage was that he would oscillate between withdrawal and frenzy. Another consequence, not mentioned in the first chapter, is that man's imagination begins to wander. The resultant judgments about his fellow man are not always generous. Once fixed in his mind, well-meaning public speech about "tolerance" and the like may mask those judgments, but it will not banish them. Only real face-to-face relations can, for a moment, stop the imagination from wandering.

> From the moment when common affairs are treated in common, each man perceives that he is not as independent of those like him as he first fancied, and that to obtain their support he most often lend them his cooperation.[24]

When all politics becomes national politics, when we less and less need to reach out to our neighbor, then political ideas need no longer be tempered or attenuated. No longer brought down to earth by the real-life compromises that neighbors must always make with one another, ideas become reified, positions harden, and, most importantly, each side begins to develop a caricatured image of the other that need never be modified.

I do not doubt that the polarization between Left and Right in America today will increase as neighbor becomes more isolated from neighbor. The Democratic and Republican parties, for their part, have only exacerbated this problem through periodic congressional redistricting that hollows out opposition and assures that those elected to their House seats need not discover a basis for conciliation or earn the trust of a broad-spectrum constituency. Once in Congress, their exercise of political judgment is often abdicated and handed over to the regulatory agencies that now constitute an ever-expanding Fourth Branch of government, which adds to the sense of impotence that citizens feel and emboldens the two political parties to entice them with even grander claims about what they can deliver.

In the Middle East, there are seemingly intractable political problems, to be sure. Polarization of the sort seen in America, however, is not one of them. In the Middle East, notwithstanding the half-century experiments with socialism, politics remains largely what it always has been—a rapprochement between the various estates that are a legacy of the aristocratic age. There may be brutal fighting but not polarization. That is largely an American phenomenon. In America, by virtue of the de-linkage that the Middle East does not yet fully know, democratic man does not really belong to a particular estate, and politics is largely fought out in the realm of interests and ideas. Insofar as man withdraws into himself and his imagination is left to wander, his ideas are unlikely to be tempered and political polarization at the national level will likely remain intense. Indeed, it will continue to grow.

The deeper question my students from the Middle East are asking, as I mentioned, is whether the American polity has become so wounded that it cannot recover. I tell them that without an understanding of the disease from which democratic man suffers, there can be no remedy, no balm for the wound. The exceptional condition from which the Americans suffer is de-linkage of the sort that no other nation in history has known. That de-linkage gives rise to many of the peculiarities in American society that my students from the Middle East observe from afar even if they don't fully understand. "It is not good for man to be alone." From that luminous beginning follows the whole of Tocqueville's healing art in *Democracy in America*. Loneliness, he assures us, need not be the final word. Bleak as the condition of the American polity can at times appear to be, it can always be renewed through face-to-face relations.

The remedy is invariably painful and will not be chosen, I suspect, until the realization dawns that the consequences of any alternative cure not involving face-to-face relations would be worse.

3 The Household: Sustenance and Reproduction

Debt and Payment

Most of my students on the main campus do not understand that they live in a world of debt and payment. So mortal life has been for all of recorded history, yet they know it not. In the beginning was debt. The Code of Hammurabi, which antedates the Ten Commandments by five centuries, is a codex of payments and compensations for transgressions great and small. A thousand years later, Plato's great masterpiece, *The Republic*, begins in earnest with a tired old man, Cephalus, declaring that justice involves paying back one's debts. The Gospel of Matthew, compiled a half century or so after Christ's death, announces that man's debt to God was so great that only the self-sending and self-sacrifice of God himself, in the person of his Son, could pay it off (Matt. 20:28). The science of economics, which was set on its current foundation with the publication of Smith's *The Wealth of Nations* in 1776, pretends to be neither cosmology, nor philosophy, nor theology; yet by presupposing scarcity, economics, too, tells us that we have lived and always will live in a world of debt and payment. So it will be, I suspect, until the end of history, when the proverbial lion finally lies down with the lamb (Isa. 11:6), gnawing scarcity is with us no more, and sustenance and reproduction are no longer the perilous undertakings they now must be.

It would be tempting to say that the reason my students on the main campus do not understand debt and payment is because they are relatively well-off. While this is true about a great many of them, I do not think that answer is very helpful. Something more profound is at work here in Tocqueville's democratic age, which invites nearly everyone—rich, poor, and all those in the middle—to lose sight of the verities of debt and payment.

We lose our bearings, in part, because the condition of social equality itself bids us to do so. This much my students have taught me. For them, no other single idea is more taken for granted and tacitly obvious than that equality should be the first idea we consider when we think about justice—or rather "social justice," as they now call it, which presupposes just this equality. The corollary, which is seldom stated and never examined, is that no one should have to endure failure.

Living in a world of debt and payment, however, entails that some will fail in a portion of life, if not in its entirety.

This prevailing incomprehension that failure is an ineradicable part of man's life hobbles my students' ability to understand all the generations that have gone before them and renders them quite incapable of thinking about the modern household in other than dreamy ways. They understand sustenance and reproduction to be without cost. While the condition of social equality may not cause their misunderstanding, it does nothing to disabuse them of their fancies. Indeed, their fancies are encouraged by it.

In Praise of Failure

I have already mentioned the traumatic events of the 1960s and how we received them on the elm tree–lined streets of Ann Arbor. As I told my eldest son more than a decade ago, on the afternoon of September 10, 2001: To witness those great upheavals in American life was to be marked indelibly and sealed as a member of the sixties generation forever.

We were not formed by these upheavals alone, however. There were the wondrous lessons of friendship, many of which have lasted a lifetime. In addition, there were the stirrings of affection that occasionally blossomed into love. In a few instances, these became the measure for all the trials and errors that followed, although we did not know it at the time. As well, in the case of my assemblage of friends, we were formed by the lessons of summer baseball. There on the Ann Arbor fields, we would compete with teams from other schools whose rosters included players with superhuman strength and courage, and whose exploits we had heard about from afar. They had, in our estimation, an almost mythical status, which redoubled in the forum of our junior high school parties, where we discussed them as do members of one tribe contemplating war against another.

Baseball is a game not for boys or for men, but for boys on their way to becoming men. That is where its most important work is done. So it was for my generation, anyway. Without much formal guidance, we had become a reasonably self-governed lot, thanks to years playing capture the flag together as dusk fell on the nearby elementary school grounds to which we returned summer after summer. It was our coach, however, who gave us guidance that by ourselves we could not have provided. As I look back, I marvel at how important my father was in giving me quiet direction and at how other men—teachers and coaches who seemed to know in advance what my next step needed to be—were no less significant for the guidance they offered.

Our baseball coach during those turbulent junior high school years held a prominent place in the University of Michigan sports pantheon, by virtue of having set eight Michigan track records and a world-record 48.1-second quarter-mile that by some accounts stood for twenty years after he ran it in 1942. In addition, he was for thirty-seven years the inimitable voice of University of Michigan football—"Meechigan football," as he would call it—on WJJX radio. A man of great humor and occasionally an irascible temperament, he demanded excellence and fidelity to the game and to the sportsmanship that gave it dignity. When we failed to measure up, we quickly heard about it. His words could be withering; yet I

don't ever recall any other sentiment than gratitude. If we suffered under his care, it never occurred to us to attend to how
badly we may have felt, since we understood our suffering to
be the price that had to be paid to achieve mastery. There was
nothing personal in his indictment, either intended or taken.
The question before us was whether we were playing in accordance with the standards established by the game of baseball.
That was all. The etiquette of base running; the intricacies of
pulling off a double play; the coordinated efforts needed to
throw a man out at the plate from deep in the outfield; how to
slide into a base without harm; what to do on an overthrow;
how to alter your step off the mound if you are throwing too
many inside or outside pitches—these challenges and dozens
more like them occupied us and our coach every minute we
were on the field. Our occasional failures, far from dissuading
us from further play, only deepened our understanding of the
standards to which we were being held and heightened our
desire to achieve them.

Years later, while at the University of Chicago writing my
dissertation, I came across a passage in Rousseau's magisterial even if maddening educational treatise, *Émile*, published
in 1762, which I doubt our coach had ever read, but with which
he would have agreed in full:

> What is to be said about these arsenals of machines set up
> around a child to arm him at all points against pain, so that
> when he is grown up he is at its mercy without courage and
> without experience, believes he is dead at the first prick, and
> faints on seeing the first drop of his blood?[1]

Young men were to be subject to tribulations, Rousseau wrote.
Pain, suffering, and failure should be our first lessons, so that
they need not be our last ones. So our baseball coach taught
us as well. Defeat was not sweeter than victory; but we did
learn enough from it so that future victories came our way. It
never could have occurred to us that we should do away with

the lessons of failure, for we knew even as teenage boys that some of us would succeed and some of us would not. That we took for granted. The justice we sought involved being given a chance to have some say about our own standing—not altering the terms of life's engagements so that failure itself would be ruled out. That breathtaking idea would have to wait for another generation to take hold: the generation my sons and my students call their own.

It would be futile to try to identify just when this belief that failure need not be a necessary part of life came to prevail. If Rousseau is any indication, the belief has been with us for some time, at least in rudimentary form. In *Democracy in America*, Tocqueville suggested that the condition of social equality would soften our hearts and our habits; he worried that in the distant future democratic man would feel overwhelmed by even the slightest challenge.

That distant prophecy is now fully upon us, I fear. Almost everywhere we look, the hard lessons of failure are ruled out. In our universities, student grades have become so inflated that they are almost meaningless. What, really, can be expected from our children if from the very moment of their birth they have been told that they are "special"? In our churches, congregations around the country hear the doctrine of universal salvation preached every Sunday. Jonathan Edwards, America's most profound theologian and author of the infamous 1741 sermon "Sinners in the Hands of an Angry God," is no doubt turning in his grave. Man's worthiness, he thought, was a gift of God and not an attribute of fallen man. And since President George H. W. Bush formally inaugurated the tradition of officially pardoning the Thanksgiving turkey at the White House in 1989, even the symbolism of our most important civic holiday has been publicly altered. However contrived, what once was a debt offering of gratitude to God that marked the end of a season of labor in life's fields has now been stripped of its significance. No debt, no sacrifice, no failure, no payment. Little wonder that when the most recent financial crisis came fully upon us in 2008, "too big to fail" came so quickly to our lips. If Rousseau is correct, our aversion to failure has only set us up for far grander failures in the future. We live in a world of debt and payment; try as we may, no sophisticated alteration of the accounting rules for the ledger of life can change that.

When my sons were young, it seemed fitting that I repay the debt I owed to my coach by helping the next generation find its way on the baseball field. Sometimes transfer payments are the only way debts can be repaid. Eager to pass on the lessons my generation had learned, I soon discovered that most of the mothers and some of the fathers in the bleachers had other ideas. Every play was greeted with the choral chant, "Good job." When I explained that our boys needed to learn the difference between success and failure on the field in order to be victorious, both in play and in life, it was suggested that we not tell them the score at all, for fear it would hurt their feelings if they lost. At the end of this season without bearings, there were trophies for all. And I remembered Rousseau's words.

The End of History

I am not surprised, then, that many of my students today are discomforted by the notion that failure is an irrevocable aspect of life. Even when their minds reluctantly accede to the importance of the idea, the habits their parents have instilled quickly steer them in another direction.

I mentioned in chapter 1 that not long after the Cold War ended in 1989, my students on the main campus may have had some dreamy ideas in the classroom about what communism offered, but they did not really much believe them once they graduated. A generation later, a certain feature of Marx's thinking has more appeal now than it did at the end of the Cold War, even while the whole of his thinking remains largely foreign to them. Today many of my students believe that they live in a world in which the struggle and competition of the "capitalist" phase of history is now behind us, and that all that remains to be done is redistribute the existing wealth so that "social justice" prevails.

In *The Manifesto of the Communist Party*, Marx had coined a phrase for this sort of thinking: "bourgeois socialism." Bourgeois socialists, he argued,

> want all the advantages of modern social conditions without the struggles and dangers necessarily resulting therefrom. They desire the existing state of society, minus its revolutionary and disintegrating elements. They wish for a bourgeoisie without a proletariat.[2]

It is not hard to imagine why my students today are enthralled with this sort of thinking, which has for them become almost habitual. They nod knowingly when the litany against "capitalism" is rehearsed—the inequality it produces, the competition it invites, the cleavages it fosters, the straightforward ascription of guilt and innocence that different social classes deserve. Yet without knowing it, they inhabit a world that Marx derided. The riddle of history, Marx wrote, can only be solved when scarcity is finally overcome. All of history up to that point is a struggle with nature and a struggle between men. The belief that failure is no longer necessary may make sense *after* the revolution, but not before. Before the revolution, "capitalism" ruthlessly weeds out those who cannot compete and destroys those who want to rest contentedly and self-assuredly where they are.

My students are drawn to Marx, then, because of his vision of the end of history, which they think is now upon us, and which their upbringing has prepared them to embrace. Gone is the need for competition and failure and the inequality they produce. That is why so many of them may properly be called bourgeois socialists. Their indictment of "capitalism" is that it is an anachronism (not unlike traditional religion, some would say, which once served its purpose but is now obsolete). When pressed, however, they know little of Marx's larger theoretical apparatus: the tension between essence and existence, which only history finally resolves; the nature of dialectical change; the necessity, therefore, of comprehending history in terms of definitive stages; the need to specify the original human condition as one of innocence, among other matters. They neither know nor care to know about this larger theoretical apparatus because their life has taught them, simply, that equality should prevail and that failure should be ruled out. Marx's vision of a post-historical epoch after "capitalism" provides them with a way to dimly conceptualize that. They rely on Marx but are not Marxists; for they want "social justice," not revolution. They think of themselves as heralds of the future and in this way resemble Marx's vanguard of the proletariat. They are not Marxists, however. They are democratic souls of the sort Tocqueville thought would someday appear.

Market Commerce

Because failure cannot, in fact, be eradicated, I introduce my students to Smith's *The Wealth of Nations*, a book without the fanciful illusion that animates much of Marx's thinking. The first thing I tell them is that Smith never used the term "capitalism." That term supposes that there are distinct stages in history—something Smith did not really believe. Above all, Smith did not believe that we will ever arrive at a historical moment when scarcity will come to an end. Competition is unending; the best we can do is to organize competition so that it can bring about "improvement," as he would call it.[3] Not yet willing to step into Smith's world, my students are quick to point out that "capitalism" is based on greed. I tell them that greed, like competition, has been with us for all of human history, and that Smith sought to channel it rather than pretend he could eradicate it, as Marx fancied he himself would.

The second thing I tell them is that Smith was battling against an inherited understanding of both commerce and wealth that had been in place for a very long time. Even in

Smith's day, commerce was largely carried on through guilds, which were granted exclusive prerogatives over this or that craft. Guild membership was often a family affair, or something this stratum of society could undertake, but not that one. Social mobility was, consequently, nearly non-existent. Wealth, in turn, was thought to be best measured in terms of accumulated gold and silver—which helps us understand one of the reasons that the New World was pillaged by European nations during the seventeenth and eighteenth centuries.

Smith's great insight about commerce and wealth was that they can be best understood on the basis of what Tocqueville, in *Democracy in America*, would later call the "two new axioms of industrial science,"[4] namely, the division of labor and the extensiveness of markets. Based on these two axioms, Smith concluded that the closed guild system was an obstacle to improving man's lot, and that accumulated gold and silver were not the true measure of the wealth of nations.

It is hard for my students to understand the world that Smith inhabited: the guild system of production is largely gone; they would, moreover, find it odd if their government claimed that nations were wealthy because of the amount of gold and silver held in national banks. They use the term "gross domestic product" without thinking about it, yet don't realize that Smith was the first one to introduce the idea, in the opening paragraph of *The Wealth of Nations*. In their own lives, they take for granted that one of the reasons they are going to college is to develop generic "skills" that help them compete on the "job market." These ideas would have no referent in the world Smith himself inhabited: the guild system reproduced itself in its own image, through apprenticeships. The modern system of market commerce that Smith's ideas help inaugurate, on the other hand, perpetually introduces novelty, which is why colleges and universities must graduate students who can be trained to do nearly anything after they graduate, but who are not really trained for anything when they receive their diploma. My students accept the current arrangement without questioning how it came about. They do not know that Smith's ideas have constituted a large part of the world they comfortably inhabit yet claim to reject.

Smith's two axioms of industrial science are introduced in *The Wealth of Nations* in his now-famous example of the pin maker. When one man or a group of men work together in a small shop to manufacture pins, each is involved in all or most of the steps necessary to fabricate them. Each man makes a few pins well, but together they produce only a modest number of pins per day. If each man, however, turns his attention to just one phase of the production of pins—if, in other words, there is a strict division of labor—then the total number of pins produced each day by the same number of men increases enormously.

This vast increase in productivity cannot be justified, however, unless there is a market for the large number of pins that the division of labor produces. That is why the division of labor and the extensiveness of markets go hand in hand. Only an increase in the size of the market can justify a more differentiated division of labor. With the discovery of the Americas and their integration into the European economy, markets expanded and the division of labor that Smith described began to develop in earnest. The improvements of the past several centuries, on which my students rely, have occurred in part because of this correlative development of the division of labor and expanding markets.

Establishing the Price

These two axioms of industrial science alone are not enough to bring about improvement, however. Beyond these, there must be a mechanism for private capital to move from place to place so that it can be put to profitable use—something that cannot occur without being able to establish the natural price of a product or a service.

In every corner of the world, of course, products and services have prices. In the Middle East, as is well known, prices can generally be haggled over. "For you, special price," as the old saying goes. Moreover, because of various privileges and protections that the state grants to prominent families, the natural price of a product or service is virtually unknown, if not unknowable. Whether in an open-air market or in a shopping center, the vexing question is the same: Does the price declared have any traceable relationship to the cost of producing what is being purchased? I suspect this is one of the reasons why haggling occurs in the first place: absent any firm knowledge of the real cost of what is being sold, the proprietor simply tries to get the most he can. He often has no carefully worked-out projections based on the real and anticipated costs of labor, materials, and rent; no intention of charging each and every customer just slightly less than what competitors are charging; no cleared path to further develop the business that does not entail some helpful interposition by state agents or agencies; no assurance that proceeds need not be shared with the patron who allows the business owner to open and remain in business in the first place. Why should he not simply to get whatever high price he can from this unknowing customer?

In the United States, the situation is generally reversed. Prices are usually clearly marked. They change, to be sure, but rarely because of negotiations at the point of sale. Rather, as the prices of the components of the product or service change, the shelf cost, so to speak, of the next shipment or delivery is altered accordingly. The natural price is generally known, and the margin of profit or loss can be ascertained in advance of the sale. When the natural price is not known, earnest efforts are made to establish just what it is. Business in America, after all, must operate by the numbers—so much so that the product or service offered seems sometimes of lesser concern than the numbers that their sales generate. Here, the economy of obligation and loyalty seems to be ephemeral. Wealth, it is purported, always has a measure. The business and personal finance software programs that assist in its creation have no asset or debit class called "obligation and loyalty" encoded into their algorithms. (That class of payments nevertheless inevitably resides in the interstices of almost every business operation—though in vain does the clerk and the accountant attempt to establish its numerical value. Notwithstanding democratic man's valiant effort, the economy whose currency of money, it seems, can never completely supplant the economy whose currency is obligation and loyalty.)

There is much to be gained when every product and service has a price—and something that is lost, as well. Many of my students from the Middle East are perplexed when they enter a shop in America and discover that prices are not negotiable or that tea will not be served before the business of haggling over the price commences. They conclude that business in America is a cold and calculated affair, notwithstanding the friendliness of the employees who greet them. My American students, on the other hand, are generally surprised by how lavish even the poorest shopkeeper in the Middle East can be, with his time and with his tea. They wonder whether he understands just how precarious his operation is. And even if he mercilessly extracts more money from them than the object he sells is worth, my students sometimes leave feeling as if they have still made out better than he has, by virtue of their knowledge of how a *real* business should operate, which he does not have. They do not realize that he stays in business partly from the money he earns and partly because the hidden economy of obligation and loyalty protects him from the failure that my American students are convinced awaits him. Those above and below him both owe and receive obligation and loyalty. That is largely the reason his shop doors open each morning.

My students from the Middle East understand this. That is why they think American business is cold and calculated. They do not think money alone can be the currency that holds a society together and are incredulous when Americans, on both the Left and the Right, declare that the troubles of the Middle

East can be attributed, in part, to the absence of "free markets." Lacking the voluntary civic habits in American society that counterbalance the market commerce found there, my Middle Eastern students are left to wonder what kind of society they would really have if, as Marx called it, "callous cash payment" was the only currency available to them, if the ties of obligation and loyalty were irretrievably severed. They are not alone in this apprehension: every European anti-modern thinker since Rousseau has grappled with this problem in terms of just these oppositions. In America, however, the ties of obligation and loyalty were never strong, and the existence of vibrant civic habits that substitute for them meant that society was held together by more than "callous cash payment." My discussion below about what is gained through market commerce presupposes those attenuating civic habits.

Improvement

When money becomes the measure, when the natural price of a product or a service can be ascertained and given a numerical value, then capital can, in principle, flow to where it will be put to good use, and "improvement" can occur. This can happen, however, only if businesses actually have to shutter their doors when their money runs out. If there is to be "improvement," there must be failure. In the words of one prominent economist: "[Market commerce] without failure is like religion without sin—it just doesn't work."

Many of my Middle Eastern students are reluctant to take this course. They live in an honor culture, a face-saving culture; and few things more offend their imagination than the idea that for their lot to be markedly improved, they must be willing to endure the prospect of humiliation and public failure. Almost any American who has spent time in the Middle East trying to create an organization knows well the difficulty of getting a reliable answer from the governing authorities on how to proceed. That is because rather than dismantle broken portions of the governing apparatus, which would bring shame to the authorities in charge, new edifices are built alongside the old ones, which have roughly the same purview. This sort of Venn-diagram governance, if you will, is endemic in the Middle East and occurs in large measure because politics, and economics too, is understood within the framework of honor and face-saving rather than of transparency and efficiency—the latter of which pairings presuppose that failure must be exposed and routed out.

When my Middle Eastern students read passages from Smith's *The Wealth of Nations* that argue without dismay that business failures are a necessary aspect of market commerce, they cannot help but think about the dishonor involved. That thought never seemed to occur to Smith. Nominal Presbyterian that he was, his attentiveness to the religious sequence of sin and redemption, of fault and atonement, meant that he could have little patience for the constellation of honor and face-saving, which Christianity from the beginning made every effort to repudiate. I suspect, but cannot prove, that this is why his economic thought so scrupulously ignores the central inconvenience that my Middle Eastern students find in his work. My American students on the main campus, as I have mentioned, are increasingly uneasy about Smith's thinking, because failure does not accord with the habits of mind their parents have instilled in them since birth. The reason for the suspicion that each group evinces about Smith's thinking may be different, but their conclusion is the same: they do not want a world in which failure and success, like the wheat and tares (Matt. 13:24–30, 36–43), are necessarily intertwined.

I ask them, nevertheless, to set aside this trepidation about failure and imagine how market commerce works and how it can yield "improvement." If the natural price of a product or service can be known, and if there are buyers willing to pay a price higher than the natural price, then the enterprise offering that product or service earns a profit. Assuming there are no barriers to entry, as economists call them, other entrepreneurs may choose to put their capital to work and compete with the enterprise that is already making a profit. The new entrant may do well for a while, but soon the extra supply of the product or service that both of them together provide will not find enough buyers, and the price will fall. This will force both enterprises to lower their price and find more efficient ways of delivering the product or service. Should the market price fall below the natural price, one or the other of the enterprises will eventually shut its doors and go out of business. Not supported by the economy of obligation and loyalty, success or failure hinges on whether the market price is above or below the natural price.

In principle, this perpetual fluctuation of market price around natural price is a transparent affair, which allows entrepreneurs to decide where their capital should be directed. If there is no money to be made, capital will be redirected; if there is money to be made, other entrepreneurs can be expected to develop kindred products and services of their own. Enterprises that are poorly run will go out of business; enterprises that are able to do ever more with less, that innovate, will succeed. This never-ending competition, in which there are no foreordained winners and in which entrepreneurs must perpetually look over their shoulders at the competition, rousts man from his slumber and does not allow him any self-satisfaction with the present state of things. Dreams of wealth fire his imagination and lead to the development of novel products and services, most of which will fail. A few, however, will transform the material world and assist democratic man in his restless and never-ending search for "well-being"—a term that Tocqueville uses throughout *Democracy in America*—which is the chief aspiration in the democratic age.

The Problem of Excessive Profit

Many of my students on the main campus, as I have said, are troubled by this depiction of market commerce—though not with the result of its workings. The prospect of failure offends their democratic sensibilities. That is not all. The fact of profit-making affronts their understanding of justice itself. They point to enterprises that make large profits and think them either "unfair" or morally odious. I tell them that an economy based on market commerce would never tolerate large profits for long, since large profits earned would signal other entrepreneurs that their capital would be put to good use just there.

The offense within an economy based on market commerce is not that large profits *are* made; the offense, I tell them, is that large profits *continue* to be made.

If large profits continue to be made year after year, that is a sign not of the success of market commerce, but rather a sign that something has gone seriously awry. It is a sign that an enterprise has been protected by political agents or agencies, or by some convention, so that no other entrepreneur can compete with it and, therefore, lower both the market price and the profit margin of the product or service. Alternatively, it is a sign that the barriers to entry are so large that no other entrepreneur dare risk his capital to try to compete.

When Smith wrote *The Wealth of Nations*, the larger problem was that various enterprises—guilds—received protections from political agents or agencies. In our day, often because of the sophistication of the technology involved and, consequently, the regulatory oversight sometimes needed to assure that it does not go awry, the greater problem is the barrier to entry. If enterprises are confronted with the need to conform to regulatory burdens when competition is acute, they are apt to vigorously protest. As those enterprises grow larger, however, they will often welcome such burdens—for nothing assures their continuing dominance than the addition of regulatory requirements, the costs of which they can absorb and pass on because of their commanding position in the market, but which prospective entrants to their market could not think of paying for.

This helps explain, for example, why so many large-scale enterprises in America have "gone green" when conventional thinking would suggest that they would be reluctant to do so: whenever more stringent and costly environmental regulations go into effect, they know that adhering to them will all but guarantee that they will have fewer and fewer competitors in the long run. Whatever else their benefits may be, the same calculation is involved when it comes to financial regulations, affirmative action requirements, or any other government-mandated constraint. Why struggle to expand market share with innovative products and services when ever-increasing government regulations will eliminate the competition for you?

It is not just large enterprises that benefit from higher barriers to entry; political agents or agencies do so as well. As the barriers to entry increase and the remaining enterprises grow and have fewer competitors, those enterprises look to political agents or agencies to assure that the rules under which they operate either will not be altered at all or changed in accordance with the wishes of those enterprises. The pace of "improvement" thereby slows, huge fortunes are made, patronage politics becomes the order of the day, and the middle class, more than any other, suffers.

The Dream of "Economic Justice"

When my students on the main campus describe the problems facing America today, they are generally not apt to wonder how market commerce has been circumvented; rather, their impulse is to believe that the economic injustice they purport to witness can best be addressed through more stringent regulation of large and successful enterprises. They do not see that alongside the good that such regulations may bring, these regulations also tighten the bond between those enterprises and the political agents and agencies that ostensibly oversee and guide them. In the midst of the constant change that both entrances and exhausts man in the democratic age, this vision of economic justice through more stringent regulation invariably produces a permanent class of winners and losers—both economic and political.

My students recognize that this is happening yet do not often understand that the solution they propose is implicated in bringing the problem they see about in the first place. Market commerce, I tell them, involves managing risk for the purpose of making profit and risking failure along the way. When political agents or agencies step in to regulate large enterprises, the risk to which such enterprises are exposed thereby diminishes but the profits often do not. In some circumstances, in fact, the calculation of risk changes entirely: rather than *managing* risk, the assurance of political protection leads them to *take* risks. When this occurs, an enterprise knows that it is "too big to fail" and that the losses it may generate will be shifted to the public balance sheet. This is not market commerce.

The economy of obligation and loyalty found in the aristocratic age, I remind my students, assures a measure of balance between long-established families, classes, tribes, or castes. (The vestiges of "socialism" in Europe are probably best thought of in this light—as an ongoing compact between the various "estates" within society.) The arrangements found there may shift to and fro, but for the most part those arrangements ensconce permanent winners and losers. Nothing like that is thinkable for Americans in the democratic age. Here, man does not think of himself preeminently as a member of a family, class, tribe, or caste. On his own, his charge is to make his way in an uncertain world, relying largely on his own ambition and his ability to bring to bear the resources he has at his command in order to secure well-being. The conditions of social equality no doubt militate against the idea that failure is a necessary part of life. So, too, those conditions lead democratic man to be dubious about great inequalities of wealth and about the profits that make those inequalities possible—as the recent Occupy Wall Street movement attests. These sentiments invite the mind to consider the daring plan of equalizing fortunes altogether. Troubled that equality of *opportunity* yields inconvenient disparities, the mind ponders whether equality of *outcome* is the final and true condition of democratic justice.

I do not think, however, that these considerations can finally captivate the democratic imagination, not least because the political and economic manipulations that would be necessary to accomplish this sort of justice, such as it is, would produce a permanent administrative class of winners who would hover over the great mass of equalized, democratic subjects and inadvertently halt the material progress that market commerce makes possible. If equality of outcome is the goal, it is conceivable for a time that democratic man will endure being ruled by an administrative class that strips him of his freedom to succeed or to fail. He will not, however, long submit to that arrangement because of the restlessness in his heart that no political arrangement can fully snuff out. That restlessness may well have a deeper cause than the anxieties the democratic age produces. Proximally, however, it can be largely assuaged by the improvements that market commerce makes possible.

The paradox of the democratic age is that the very commitment to equality, which seems to repudiate the nearly permanent social arrangements of the aristocratic age, can easily generate political and economic measures that produce a new kind of permanent inequality—this time not between families, classes, tribes, or castes but between masters and subjects. With or without consent, an administrative class might well impose equality on its subjects, but such an arrangement will not lead to well-being—that ineffable admixture of material comfort and personal satisfaction that is man's aspiration in the democratic age. Important as equality surely is, the passion for well-being is, I suspect, more deeply rooted in the human heart. Suspending the mechanisms of market commerce can temporarily satisfy the mind that longs for equality; but only market commerce proper, with its necessary successes and failures, can satisfy the heart's long-term desire for well-being.

Many of my students on the main campus will declare that they want equality. They are not prepared, however, to give up their longing for the latest technological innovation or their belief that their worldly success will exceed the level that their fathers and mothers achieved. I doubt that a political party that does not understand that democratic man's desires are equivocal, and which fights above all for an equality of outcome, will long hold sway over the democratic imagination. Indeed, when a political party takes hold of the economy in the name of helping to bring about an equality of outcome, its policies will, in the long run, impoverish the nation. As I write this, the current underemployment crisis in America has, for example, elicited from both political parties declarations that "jobs" must be "created." Jobs that are not mere make-work cannot be created, however, unless something of value is produced. Value, in turn, cannot be produced unless the natural price of a new product or service can be ascertained and compared to existing products and services. Yet the never-ending political intercession by both parties into market commerce has made it quite difficult to establish the natural price of all too many products and services. No natural price, no value; no value, no jobs. Sometimes "helping" doesn't.

Tocqueville's Caveats

I mentioned at the outset of the last section that I acquaint my students on the main campus with Smith's *The Wealth of Nations* so that they might begin to question their habituated belief that failure should be eradicated. Tocqueville certainly understood that the market commerce Smith advocated would help democratic man in his never-ending search for well-being. His endorsement of market commerce was qualified, however, by his understanding of the peculiar social conditions that would attend the democratic age. Tocqueville's thinking about market commerce must be understood in that light.

For market commerce to work, the economy of obligation and loyalty must have largely broken down, and money must have become the measure of business success or failure. The corresponding social condition that obtains is the one that Tocqueville thinks characterizes man's situation in the democratic age: lonely, delinked, and homeless in an ever-changing world. His thinking about market commerce begins with the fact of this loneliness and de-linkage, and addresses itself to the question of how market commerce may ease the anxious condition of democratic man.

In the aristocratic age, social standing assures that some will seldom worry about losing what they have, and most will never dream of gaining more than what their current misfortune allows. The former have time for leisure and high culture; the latter find solace in the world to come. When, in the democratic age, everyone is ill-assured of their place in society, when each man has enough to taste of the blessings of prosperity but not enough to be certain that he will retain what he has, material life becomes a source of continuing anxiety, and market commerce becomes immensely more important. Membership in the middle class, which a vast majority of Americans claim as their own, is probably best characterized by just this sort of anxiety. Along with the fixation on money, it is one of the central features of the democratic age. So deep does this anxiety run, in fact, that no political party will ever successfully convince the American citizenry that they can be delivered from it by supporting them, try as it may.

This anxiousness casts a peculiar shadow over everything in America and even alters the framework within which market commerce is undertaken. As Tocqueville put the matter:

In the United States, a man carefully builds a dwelling in which to pass his declining years, and he sells it while the roof is being laid; he plants a garden and he rents it out just as he was going to taste its fruits; he clears a field and he leaves to the others the care of harvesting its crops. He embraces a profession and quits it. He settles in a place from which he departs soon after so as to take his changing desires elsewhere. Should his private affairs leave him some respite, he immediately plunges into the whirlwind of politics. And when toward the end of a year filled with work some leisure still remains to him, he carries his restive curiosity here and there within the vast limits of the United States. He will thus go five hundred leagues in a few days in order better to distract himself from his happiness.[5]

Little has changed. Inwardly anxious democratic man will always be outwardly impatient with the current state of things. In his business dealings, he is therefore apt to think of short-term results. This is one of the reasons why Tocqueville thought that Americans so readily left agriculture and took up an industrial calling: to wait and watch their crops grow before receiving payment at the end of the season required a patience they did not possess.

In our own day, we might add that Americans are not even patient enough to hold fast to an industrial calling and so have moved increasingly into finance, where instead of forming an enterprise or working in one for wages, they now invest in an enterprise for capital gains—preferably dispensed on a quarterly basis. This can be wholesome and helpful for both the enterprise and the investor, of course; but worth pondering is whether the next step in the contraction of patience—wherein investors become day traders and, finally, high-frequency traders—definitively alters the once-salutary role of capital. For market commerce to bring about improvement, capital must flow to enterprises that produce actual products or services. These, in turn, must enter the market so that it may be discovered whether they successfully bring about well-being. That takes time. Capital flow that is not involved in that long and patience-demanding sequence may bring profit, but it does not produce wealth. I suspect Tocqueville would have recoiled at the impatience of current-day democratic man and marveled that he had twisted the arrangements of market commerce so much so that money ceased to produce wealth. When I first arrived at Georgetown nearly two decades ago, many of my students wanted to be doctors and lawyers; today the balance has shifted, and many want to go into "financial services" — that euphemism for making money without producing anything. They are anxious and do not understand that their impatience unwittingly guides them toward the career path they think they want.

For market commerce to bring about improvement, democratic man must be patient enough to wait and see if his capital has really been put to good use. Tocqueville thought that such patience did not come naturally and, therefore, had to be formed. The discipline of market commerce can, under the best of circumstances, help instill the patience that is needed; but by itself, it cannot stop the relentless contraction of patience and of attention spans in the democratic age, which my students confirm is now upon us. Tocqueville thought, in fact, that patience *for* market commerce had to be formed elsewhere than *in* commercial activity. Insofar as it is concerned with the long and arduous task of reproduction, the family can bring a measure of patience to fathers and mothers, sons and daughters. Weekly church attendance, too, can assist: liturgical rituals remind democratic man that his world is deeper and more mysterious than the din and turmoil his senses witness; sermons, in turn, unwittingly teach him that the forbearance necessary for admission into heaven is also the secret to success in this world below.

A Role for the Federal Government

Perhaps most interesting of all, in *Democracy in America* Tocqueville thought that the federal government had a role to play in helping to form patience among citizens. This is all the more remarkable in light of his apprehension about the growing purview of the state in the democratic age. Nevertheless, he thought that the federal government ought to commit itself to long-term projects with a view to the indirect benefit such projects might have on the American character. With this idea in view, I tell my students how the space program of the 1960s really did captivate the imagination of a generation, and how we watched and anticipated each careful advance along the way, beginning with President Kennedy's speech on September 12, 1962:

> We choose to go to the moon. We choose to go to the moon in this decade and do the other things, not because they are easy, but because they are hard, because that goal will serve to organize and measure the best of our energies and skills, because that challenge is one that we are willing to accept, one we are unwilling to postpone, and one which we intend to win.

The speech seemed almost reckless at the time. On May 5, 1961, Alan Shepard, strapped to a Mercury-Redstone rocket, had become the first American to make a suborbital flight. On February 20, 1962, just seven months before President Kennedy's speech, John Glenn had become the first American to actually orbit the earth, in a capsule not much larger than a phone booth. A moon landing by the end of the decade seemed an impossibly distant goal.

Unmanned *Gemini* test flights on April 8, 1964, and January 19, 1965, only whetted our appetite for the next manned mission, which occurred on March 23, 1965, when a Titan II rocket propelled Gus Grissom and John Young skyward on *Gemini 3*. This was followed by *Gemini 4*, a four-day mission that began on June 3, 1965, with James McDivitt and Edward White, who carried out the first American space walk. Not long afterward, the two astronauts received a hero's welcome at the University of Michigan, where McDivitt had received his engineering degree six years earlier. It was a celebration of science, national purpose, and man's aspiration to explore the universe. The plaque placed just next to the engineering building commemorated their mission and reminded us of the many small but important accomplishments that would be necessary before man could step foot on the moon.

The next eight manned *Gemini* missions—*Gemini 5* on August 21, 1965; *Gemini 7* on December 4, 1965; *Gemini 6A* on December 15, 1965; *Gemini 8* on March 16, 1966; *Gemini 9* on June 3, 1966; *Gemini 10* on July 18, 1966; *Gemini 11* on September 12, 1966; *Gemini 12* on November 11, 1966—developed the systems, the procedures, and the confidence needed before the *Apollo* program could be launched. Then, on January 27, 1967, a fatal fire on the ground during a test of the *Apollo* command module killed Gus Grissom, Edward White, and Roger Chaffee. The next morning I quietly walked the few blocks between my house and the plaque placed just next to the engineering building that honored McDivitt and White, and gazed upon it reverently. Sobered by the death of White and the other two astronauts, the goal of landing a man on the man before the decade was out seemed strangely nobler than it had been when President Kennedy boldly proclaimed it five years earlier. At that moment, his assassination in 1963 seemed almost sacrificial, as if it, too, were an instance of a deeper, archaic, primordial, ghastly, but necessary bond involving death and the advancement of civilization.

A year and a half would pass before the NASA engineers would authorize the first manned *Apollo* mission, on October 11, 1968. That was *Apollo 7*. On December 21, 1968, *Apollo 8* took off for the first of three dress rehearsals for the moon landing; it was notable, among other reasons, because the astronauts read passages from Genesis as they circled the moon during their Christmas Eve transmission. The reading of the biblical passages accompanied by grainy video footage of the pockmarked moon below—intimating the primordial chaos before which God said, "Let There Be Light"—was received largely without controversy. My twin sister and I fell asleep that night by the fireplace, listening to Simon and Garfunkel's *Bookends* album, pondering the greatness of our nation and its wounds that would not yet heal. On March 3, 1969, *Apollo 9* sought to establish whether the command module and lunar module could rendezvous and dock with one another, though in earth orbit. On May 18, 1969, *Apollo 10* took both modules to the moon for one last rehearsal. And, finally, on July 16, 1969, *Apollo 11* headed for the moon carrying Neil Armstrong, Buzz Aldrin, and Michael Collins. Armstrong's first words on the lunar surface — "that's one small step for a man; one giant leap for mankind" — announced that a promise had been fulfilled, and that labor and patience had redounded to the benefit of us all.

I tell this decade-long tale of the mission to the moon to my students on the main campus and in Qatar to help them understand what Tocqueville might have meant when he wrote about projects that national governments should undertake. Whatever the direct benefits such projects might offer, it was the *indirect* and immeasurable effect on democratic character with which he was really concerned. There are obvious costs and benefits to such government undertakings, and these must to be calculated. They cannot, however, be the only consideration. Even if the mission to the moon was "costly," I suspect, but cannot prove, that it helped to develop patience in a generation that otherwise would have had even less than it did. Tocqueville would not have been so reckless as to suggest that direct costs have no bearing on the question of whether to undertake a great national project; he would not, however, have been so brittle-minded as to believe that only projects with "measureable outcomes" can be justified. The character of democratic man is not, by itself, patient. Family, religion, and, to a small but not insignificant extent, national government have a part to play in helping him become more patient than he otherwise would be.

Consider the matter from another vantage point. The attentiveness of government to measurable costs and benefits alone, without consideration given to how its programs shape character, can also inadvertently encourage the impatience that is so vexing in the democratic age. When I ask my students on the main campus, nearly all of them tell me that they have purchased lottery tickets at one time or another. I tell them that Tocqueville probably would have disapproved. State lotteries raise a great deal of revenue, to be sure; but when a ticket is purchased, the owner clutches it and says silently or aloud: "Tomorrow my life will be completely different." The direct effect of lotteries is that money is raised, often for worthy projects; the indirect effect, however, is to weaken the link between present-day labor and future hope, and to teach citizens that luck is more important than patience. The Americans, Tocqueville wrote, think of life as "a game of chance."⁶ Where possible, government should be careful not to fortify this sentiment.

Property

Patience alone, however, would not be enough for market commerce to produce well-being. Among other things, property rights must also be secure. Tocqueville thought a great deal about property. Not surprisingly, he thought about it in terms of the character that property ownership helped to form rather than its direct contribution to economic growth, important as that contribution surely is. Property ownership bears on market commerce, but that is only part of the reason it is important.

My students in Qatar largely believe in property ownership but know that throughout the Middle East property can be seized by the government and expropriated, often without recourse or adequate compensation. My students on the main campus have greater assurance that their property will not be taken from them but increasingly wonder if property ownership should be entirely rethought. The financial crisis of 2008 has brought them almost to the point of declaring that the age of home ownership is over, and that the future belongs to those who rent. The declining value of homes in America contributes immensely to this view, but something deeper is at work as well. In the democratic age, Tocqueville thought that man would be tempted to hover over the world rather than condescend into it. Sensing himself to be small and with limited means to create a life that conforms to what he wistfully envisions, he would rather "keep all his options open" and make no choice at all than choose one that will, invariably, fall short of the mark his imagination has set. Because his aspirations never conform to the world as it is, every concrete situation appears to be a form of entrapment, which activates his impulse to flee.

Tocqueville thought this impulse first emerged as a social force during the French Revolution. *Democracy in America* was written in some measure to try to figure out what antidotes the Americans had discovered to ameliorate it. Property was one of them. Property ownership, as anyone who has owned property will attest, alters man's relationship to the world. In mixing his labor with the property he owns, he is apt to exercise greater care than he otherwise would, and his attention span is likely to be extended. Most importantly, his imagination is brought down to earth through the work of his hands. Like any number of citizens in America who have suffered greatly from the downturn in real estate values, some of my students on the main campus think they are better served by orienting their lives around renting rather than owning a home. Yet to wander through the several blocks around campus where they live during the school year, to see how little they care about the stewardship of homes and gardens when they have no enduring connection to them, suggests that the effect of renting on their character is not salubrious. A nation of renters is less likely to be a nation where citizens have found a way to anchor their imaginations or live, caringly, in the world of things. Property is not only good for commerce; more importantly, in Tocqueville's view, it helps to form character.

Income Inequality

Perhaps most controversially, Tocqueville thought that the conditions of social equality in the democratic age paradoxically generated disparities of the sort not witnessed in the aristocratic age. In his words:

> In aristocracies the arena of ambition is often extreme, but its boundaries are fixed. In democratic countries it ordinarily moves on a narrow field; but should it come to leave that, one would say there is no longer anything to limit it.[7]

Few passages in *Democracy in America* evoke more comment from my students, on the main campus and in Qatar. Here and in passages that follow, Tocqueville, a good friend of market commerce, suggests that in the democratic age the competition of all against all will hem in the mass of men but that the few who escape it will soar above the rest. Some of my students on the main campus think that this social fact about the democratic age is an inconvenience that can be ignored, and that they only need be guided by the economic insight that after a certain inflection point, taxing "the rich" at progressively higher rates does not generate proportionally more tax revenue. That is no doubt true. Many of my other students on the main campus point to the alarming divergence between "the rich" and "the rest." They infer that "social justice" can be achieved through redistribution. That may also be true. Yet they ignore the inconvenient economic fact that there can be little improvement in their lot unless private capital is allowed to form and be directed toward enterprises where profit can be made. The former group thinks of economic growth without regard to the social conditions of the democratic age; the latter group thinks only of the inequalities that accrue from the conditions of social equality and have little regard for economics.

My students in Qatar are no less aware of the huge inequalities of wealth in their own societies. Some believe their societies must be understood as an amalgam of families with distinct standings, whose wealth should not be taxed and whose fortunes should be allowed to pass on in their entirety from generation to generation, so that the strength and prominence their respective families now have may be maintained or increased. When I tell them that the American experiment is in large measure predicated on the belief that there can be no permanent class of winners and losers, they are dismayed. How can that be just, they wonder.

Another group of students shares the sentiment of my students from the main campus that inequality of wealth is a great scourge, which no society should have to endure. Yet their views are tempered because of the failed experiments with socialism in the Middle East during the last half-century, which almost succeeded in destroying an aristocratic inequality based on family name and which put in its place and alongside it a new class of permanent winners and losers, in some ways more brutal than its predecessors. Unlike many of my students on the main campus, they know that the attempt to forcibly institute equality invariably replaces one class of entrenched winners with another. The inequality of wealth they witness offends them, but they know from experience that the easy solutions many of my students on the main campus would institute cannot work. Nor do they believe that a supposedly pure "free market" solution will work either, since that seems only and everywhere to make the already-chosen winners in the Middle East wealthier than they already are. In short, they believe in neither European, anti-modern, socialist utopias nor in an American-style, liberal, commercial republic. Little wonder many of them dream of constituting a society from the sources of their own civilizational inheritance.

In America, as I have mentioned, my students are divided and hold two rather different views about the disparities of wealth that accrue as social conditions become more equal. Tocqueville understood that as market commerce expanded, there would be a general improvement in the lot of man as a whole, but that the gap between the richest and the poorest members of society would also increase. I suspect he would have thought that a modestly progressive tax on the wealthiest Americans would be an appropriate mechanism for assuring that the few who soar above the rest do not become a permanent class of winners. With respect to the poorest members of society, Tocqueville was more explicit: they needed to be cared for—but *not* by the state, except in times of great crisis. Wherever possible, they should be cared for by churches, which give both wealth and poverty a face, and temper the suspicion between the giver and the receiver of the gift that invariably increases when the state steps in.

To this seemingly straightforward account must be added the caveat that at the time of the writing of *Democracy in America,* the federal government collected no federal income tax nor provided for the poorest members of society. Since that time, the revenues it collects through taxation have increased exponentially, and its administrative reach has extended proportionally.

Can this level of federal taxation and spending be maintained or even increased? I began this chapter by noting that my students on the main campus do not understand that they live, and always will live, in a world of debt and payment. For that reason, they imagine that the administrative reach of the federal government really need not be curtailed, or that the revenue shortfall needed to maintain it can be collected from "the rich," a group of whom they profess not to be a part. In short, they imagine that *their* world may remain insulated from the bald fact of debt and payment. That is not going to be possible.

When asked to think more seriously about taxation, about

payments that they will actually have to make, my students on the main campus tend to understand the matter strictly in terms of "fairness," which is to be expected when equality is the idea that configures their understanding of justice. I suspect that Tocqueville would have recommended a different course. It cannot be repeated too often that he thought that the challenge of the democratic age was to help form character where it was weakest. Tax policy, too, can assist in this charge. Aside from some variant of a progressive tax already discussed, he may well have supported a mortgage deduction (because of the salutary benefit of property ownership), a deduction for charitable contributions (because not all of the business of society can be or should fall within the purview of the state), and a deduction that fathers and mothers may take for having and raising sons and daughters (because the task of society is in large part to reproduce itself). No doubt there should be other deductions as well, all to be debated and provisionally settled by legislators charged with the somber task of mediating interests and fortifying the character of citizens in the democratic age.

Commerce and the Meaning of History

When they begin to think more seriously about the taxes they themselves will have to pay and the justification for them, my students wonder aloud whether market commerce has some grander historical significance. If they must participate in it, what larger meaning does market commerce have? Tocqueville was not alone, I tell them, in thinking that it did. Indeed, the history of political thought attests to the long development of what could be called a "fable of liberalism," to which Tocqueville contributed significantly, and some variant of which nearly all my students on the main campus believe without having explicitly learned it. The grander historical significance of commerce, according to that fable, is that it is the definitive replacement for war. "Commerce is that natural enemy of all violent passions," Tocqueville tells us.[8] No matter where my students reside on the political spectrum, they believe that. They may differ on whether we have reached a point, in the developed world, when that struggle is now behind us; but they do not doubt that the way to eliminate war is through commerce. Through commerce, man's passions are redirected in a constructive way. Through commerce, man's lot is improved and his faculties are developed. Through commerce, man is tamed. Through commerce, man's cumulative labor contributes to human flourishing—if not for his own generation, then for the generations that follow.

Because my students on the main campus believe in this general account, they presume that foreign policy ought to be directed toward opening up trade and helping to develop regions of the globe where the passions of war still prevail. In the Middle East, especially, it is axiomatic for most of them that the *real* cause of the war waged under the banner of Islam is the lack of opportunity and low standards of living in the region; and no matter what evidence is adduced, they cannot be convinced that the Jihad young Muslim warriors wage against us is about religion at all. Such warriors may say—and even believe—that they are fighting in Allah's Holy Name, but that is a kind of false consciousness; the real source of their animosity is their material deprivation. That much many of my students on the main campus believe. There may be fierce disagreement among them about how to increase opportunity and raise the standard of living, but the nobility of the goal of increasing commerce in the Middle East and around the globe is uncontested. America: a nation of traders.

This vision of the meaning of commerce in the grand sweep of history is not really shared by my students in Qatar. In the fall of 2006, when American troops were mired in Iraq and it appeared that the war there would be lost, with some hesitation I asked what they thought of the American military presence to the north. The answer I received haunts me to this day. "Your President Bush is brilliant," one student said. A number

of them agreed. Curious why they might say that in light of
the evident military failure at the time, I was told that President Bush did not attack Saddam Hussein's regime because of
weapons of mass destruction or even because he wanted to
bring freedom to the region. He attacked because he knew that
the Christian civilization of the West would prevail over Islam if it could open up its deepest wound—the long-festering
animosity between Sunni and Shia Islam. Saddam Hussein's
Ba'ath party, they remind me, consolidated rule by the Sunni
minority in Iraq. Overthrowing it would bring to power the
Shia majority there and align Iraq with Shia Iran. That young
Sunni men from Saudi Arabia were in Iraq at the time attacking their ostensible allies, the Americans, only proved that the
war between Sunni and Shia Islam had already commenced.

I do not know how prevalent this view is. I raise it not to suggest that all of my students in Qatar believe it, but that a number of them do; and to point out that the idea that commerce is
woven into the grand sweep of historical events is an unexamined belief that my students on the main campus have, which
has not taken hold in the Middle East. I do not think it will. In
the Middle East, the history that matters is the history of Islam
and, more recently, the history of Islam's encounter with the
colonial powers that have subdued or "occupied" the region.
My American students cannot understand this, in no small
part because while they may believe in God, they are largely
content to let him appear in their places of worship on his appointed day, and there alone. Wracked by anxiety about losing whatever material security they now have, and believing
that through commerce they will find the respite they seek,
most of their time and attention is fixed on it. Little wonder
history itself is purported to be organized around commerce.
Augustine would have been mystified. The vastly different
ideas about the meaning of history that my students on the
main campus and in Qatar exhibit will, I suspect, be an ongoing source of profound misunderstanding.

The Current Exhaustion

Vexing as these misunderstandings will surely be, there is also reason to be concerned by an internal deterioration of the religious understanding of history in the Muslim world, on the one hand, and by the exhaustion of the fabulous liberal account of commerce in the West, on the other. I will consider the latter here.

I mentioned earlier in the chapter that many of my students on the main campus believe that we have reached a point where in the developed world the struggle to achieve material security is now, in principle, behind us; and that without great exaggeration they may, invoking Marx's terminology, be called bourgeois socialists. They believe, as the "fable of liberalism" suggests, that the meaning of history revolves around commerce, but think that that history has now come to an end.

The "fable of liberalism," however, proposes no such resting point. What, then, is to be made of this growing reluctance among my students on the main campus to accept that our world will never offer a permanent resting place and that our future is as yet unknown? I fear that what we are witnessing is more than just a peculiarity of the current generation.

Taking the longer view, a remarkable pattern emerges. At the end of the aristocratic age several centuries ago, it was taken for granted in almost every field of knowledge that the world was characterized by stasis or cyclical patterns, not linear or dialectical development. In the 1758 edition of *Systema Naturæ*, Carolus Linnaeus had presumed a well-ordered and stable world containing creatures that can be classified in a rational taxonomic scheme. A century later, in 1859, Charles Darwin published his *On the Origin of Species*, which presumed a changing, evolving, world of nature, in which new species emerge and are extinguished through the process of natural selection. In the realm of the social sciences, the same general trend can be observed: relatively static understandings of society give way to open-ended ones, many of which exhibited confidence that an unknown but beneficent future justified the labor and suffering of the current moment. Surveying these developments together, it could be said that near the end of the aristocratic age, man still thought in terms of necessity and constraint, and that as the democratic age dawned and conditions of social equality began to emerge, man began to liberate himself from the constraint of necessity and thought in terms of open-ended freedom. In Tocqueville's words:

> As the former barriers that separated the crowd from renown and power are suddenly lowered, an impetuous and universal movement of ascent is made toward this long-envied greatness, whose enjoyment is finally permitted. In this first exaltation of triumph, nothing seems impossible to anyone.[9]

A third moment seems now to have emerged fully into the light of day, however, which Tocqueville predicted would occur as the competition of all against all exhausted democratic man and diminished his aspirations.

> People believe that the new societies are going to change face daily, and I am afraid that in the end they will be too unchangeably fixed in the same institutions, the same prejudices, the same mores, so that they human race will stop and limit itself; that the mind will fold and refold itself around itself eternally without producing new ideas, that man will exhaust himself in small, solitary, sterile motions, and that, while constantly moving, humanity will no longer advance.[10]

It is not surprising, therefore, that so many of my students on the main campus are not able to abide the opened-ended vision of an unknown future proffered by the "fable of liberalism." Exhausted, indeed frightened, by the prospect of a future the contours of which they can, at best, dimly intimate, many of them want to believe that they have arrived at the end of history, at which point the task that remains is to redistribute wealth so that "social justice" may be achieved. That is not all. The sentiment of finality that informs their thinking about the social world spills over into their understanding of the natural world that sustains them. It is axiomatic for my students on the main campus that nature is fragile and unable to accommodate another great industrial and manufacturing leap forward, because it will bring about climate change. I suspect that Tocqueville would think that these two developments—the desire to implement "social justice" and the aspiration to halt climate change—are not unrelated. In the aristocratic age, he tells us, the world is understood in terms of limits. As the democratic age dawns, the world is conceived of in terms of unbounded freedom. As equality comes to prevail, the world seems to contract and is made smaller, less forgiving, and less robust, in proportion, as democratic man's assessment of himself adjusts and becomes smaller, less forgiving, and less robust. Unable any longer to bear the burden of living with the terrifying prospect of freedom, which I suspect can only be borne when the yoke of moral responsibility is lightened by hope, democratic man returns to the warm hearth and comfortably captivity of necessity and constraint. Market commerce, in his estimation, is too hazardous for the environment to bear and poses a danger of failure too great for man himself to endure—hence the emergence of so-called "rights" designed to safeguard both the environment and democratic man from its perils. The call for "sustainable development" encompasses both.

This will not end well. In the aristocratic age, Tocqueville wrote, "the legislator claims to promulgate eternal laws [with a view to] sparing future generations the care of regulating their destinies."[11] Under the sway of our newly discovered constraints in the democratic age, I fear we can expect those same beneficent impulses from our rulers, who will assure us that the laws and regulations they enact, and the rights they extend, are intended to protect us from ourselves. Spared from the moral obligation that the call to stewardship places on us, the rise of the oceans will begin to slow, our planet will begin to heal, and the horror of Darwinian species extinction will no doubt come to an end. Perhaps even a new, post-Darwinian biology will be discovered. Spared from the moral reflection that failure can occasion, we need no longer search our souls and be deepened by our invariably painful ruminations about culpability. Then perhaps the irksome language of religion, which gives depth and breadth to those ruminations, need not trouble us either.

Tocqueville did not doubt that democratic man would someday arrive at this point of exhaustion, where each step into the unknown future would have both the mind and the heart allied against it. He hoped, nevertheless, that although "the past no longer [sheds] light on the future, and the mind advances in darkness,"[12] democratic man would not succumb.

I do not think I am off the mark in noting this general exhaustion among my students. Not all of them exhibit this, to be sure; but enough of them do so that we should be concerned. They are, of course, busy and are animated by any number of immediate concerns. More at issue is the range of their ambitions, the scope of their longings. Their energy may be no different than that of earlier generations, but it seems confined within a smaller space, more directed toward an achievable goal, more prosaic and less poetic than it should be if life is to be refreshed and renewed. I cannot imagine that this state of affairs can continue into the indefinite future.

The Reproduction of Society

In the remaining pages of this chapter, I turn from the subject of the generation of wealth to the subject of the reproduction of society. That is, I turn from commerce to the family. In order to introduce it in the brightest light possible, I return to a point I made in a previous section—that Tocqueville probably would have believed there should be a modestly progressive tax on wealth in America. I mentioned at the time that my students on the main campus are quite divided over this issue. That is so because as I write this, the dispassionate question about what general principle should prevail with respect to wealth and taxation has been overshadowed by the impassioned question of how the staggering debt that the federal government now owes can be repaid.

The gravity of this question is magnified by the fact that the looming threat of a deepening global financial crisis has all but ruled out further Keynesian stimulus measures unless additional revenues can be collected by the federal government to offset their cost. The Democratic Party is arguing that the "animal spirits" about which John Maynard Keynes wrote in his 1936 treatise, *The General Theory of Employment, Interest and Money*, can only be stirred by more federal spending, underwritten by greater taxation of wealthy citizens and cash-rich corporations. The Republican Party is arguing that the problem America faces is not one of subjective mood but of objective debt, which can only be reduced by diminishing the size and scope of the federal government to the limits set for it by the American Constitution. Oriented by Friedrich von Hayek's 1944 classic, *The Road to Serfdom*, the Republican Party imagines that this is the moment that Keynesian domestic economic policy can be put to its final rest.

The fiscal debt incurred by the federal government is indeed staggering. The problem, moreover, is not limited to America. The entire developed world is engulfed by the crisis. While it is tempting to see this as a titanic philosophical debate between Keynes and Hayek, between some version of a beneficent welfare state and a free-market constitutional republic, the debt crisis that now confronts us cannot be disentangled from the prospect of imminent demographic collapse in the developed world. Absent a growing population, the cost of supporting an older generation cannot be underwritten by the younger generations that follow it: fewer children, more unpayable debt. The developing world, I suspect, will not be far behind.

It is important to position the current philosophical debate. Notwithstanding the decimation caused by the two World Wars of the early twentieth century, when Keynes and Hayek wrote in the 1930s and 1940s, thinking about world population growth among scientists and policy makers was still under the sway of Thomas Malthus, whose 1798 work, *An Essay on the Principle of Population*, had argued that population would increase exponentially while food supply could increase only arithmetically. The implication was that global starvation lay in the future unless population growth was curbed. Tocqueville, however, provides insight into why the demographic future is actually one of decline, not increase. Consequently, neither Keynes nor Hayek sheds enough light on the problem that confronts us. How do Tocqueville's ideas help us to understand this?

One of the more remarkable things about my students on the main campus is how many of them "herd" together in groups rather than break apart, publicly, into couples. Whether during the school week or on the weekend, it is the exception rather than the rule to see a young man and a young woman walking together on the main campus, lost in sustained conversation, and clearly oriented by each other alone. Tocqueville would have been disheartened but not surprised. He worried a great deal about the future of courtship and marriage, but thought the Americans of his day were a religious people of a certain sort, who had "conceived the highest and most just idea of conjugal happiness."[13]

I mentioned in the previous chapter that both ease of social relations and natural affection only fully emerge in the democratic age, and that they are generally salutary. The conditions of equality that bring them about, however, also undermine the formalities that choreograph the relations between the sexes. Equal and without the benefit of the protocols through which a man and a woman may diminish but never wholly overcome their misunderstandings and civilize their longing for one another, my students have been taught that there are no natural differences between men and women around which durable roles can be formed. As Tocqueville put the matter:

> There are people in Europe who, confusing the diverse attributes of the sexes, intend to make of man and woman beings not only equal, but alike. They give both the same functions, impose the same duties on them, and accord them the same rights; they mix them in all things—labor, pleasures, affairs.[14]

This depiction now generally prevails in America, at least in publicly encouraged understandings. What Tocqueville envisioned has largely come to pass: young men and women on the main campus today are taught that there is nothing natural about their sex—that they are, instead, "gendered" beings, who are what they are mostly because of the socialization they have received. I am not sure they fully believe it. Nevertheless, when they meet, it is understood that they must "negotiate" the terms of their engagement with one another. Absent roles on which to fall back, their encounters must consist in frequent contestation and not a little irony. That is one of the reasons why they herd together. Without the mediation of formalities that have all but disappeared, young men and women on campus today "date" less and less. When they do fall under each other's spell, they are reluctant to publicly declare it. Neither with each other or wholly on their own, they sometimes inhabit a nether zone of affection that invites subterfuge and seediness of the sort that daily breaks hearts and hardens them.

They herd because ease of social relations and natural affection in the democratic age make it possible to do so; they also herd because the absence of choreography makes a publicly named alternative frightening or quaint. What, really, can be expected of them if they have been taught that most if not all of their inherited conventions are anachronisms or mechanisms of oppression?

I do not doubt that they *can* be; but I also doubt that a world wholly without them is as happy as defenders of such an arrangement declare. The conditions of social equality bring about many salutary developments in the democratic age, some of which I have identified along the way. There are, however, troubling aspect of these conditions, which cannot be overlooked. My students struggle with the multiple and often confusing implications of living in the democratic age. Some aspects they openly embrace; in the matter of the relations between the sexes, however, when more than fleeting encounters are wanted, I do not think they are well-served by the understanding that most readily come into their minds. Alas, in the democratic age, there is a great longing for a parsimony that never arrives.

When social equality prevails and the relations between the sexes must be perennially renegotiated because roles have been repudiated, it is almost inevitable that young men and women will look to some other purportedly reliable guide by which they should adjudge and choose each other, one not subject to the vagaries of the ever-changing social world. Many of them think they find the knowledge they seek through sexual intimacy, through erotic love.

The affinity between sexual intimacy and reliable knowledge has been chronicled since ancient times. In the Hebrew Bible, Adam is said to have "known" Eve, whereupon she conceived and bore Cain (Gen. 4:1); and Plato's Socrates, ever in search of wisdom, tells us in the *Symposium* that "the only thing [he understands] is the art of love."[15] Erotic love is not the highest form that Eros can take, to be sure; but it nevertheless points to the knowledge that is needed.

So powerful is erotic love, however, that it overwhelms man unless it is disciplined, redirected, transposed, sublimated. In the Hebrew Bible and in the New Testament, erotic love is of service to man if circumscribed by the institution of marriage. For Plato, erotic love is of assistance to man if oriented by the love of wisdom. Many of my students on the main campus cannot yet imagine these affiliations, each of which, in their own way, point toward Eternity. Severed from this grander communion, the ecstasies that sexual intimacy affords are understood to reveal something peculiar and sacrosanct to and about the individual who experiences it—hence their comfort, and ours, with the term "sexual preference."

When sexual intimacy is understood to be a personal preference that gives certain knowledge of the sort that the ever-changing social world cannot possibly offer, it is likely to guide young men and women in their thinking about whom to marry. That is why almost all of my students believe that premarital sex should be accepted and encouraged. Marriage being a voluntary affair, they do not believe their parents can make the decision for them. And because natural affection leaves them almost insensible to the vagaries of class, religion, and, to a lesser extent, race, they are not apt to attend to such cues that, for better or worse, have steered marriage in the past. Their parents out of the picture and embarrassed that the vestiges of class, religion, and race even exist, they are inclined to think that marriage is finally about "compatibility," of which sexual compatibility is not an insignificant part.

Many of my students on the main campus are certainly correct in asserting that premarital sex gives them a kind of knowledge that they could not attain if they waited until after they were married to consummate their desires. They do not yet understand, however, that such knowledge can lead them into darkness no less than can ignorance concerning sexual compatibility. A source, simultaneously, of ethereal wonders and numberless errors, the knowledge we acquire when sexual intimacy is thought to be merely peculiar, personal, and without a more elevated significance cannot be the reliable guide my students long to find. Not yet knowing this, I worry that if they choose a spouse who turns out not to be as sexually compatible as they once thought, many of my students on the main campus are likely to begin their search anew. Aldous Huxley had imagined the final implication of this sort of thinking in his 1946 foreword to *Brave New World*:

> [The] sexual promiscuity of *Brave New World* [does not] seem so very distant. There are already certain American cities in which the number of divorces is equal to the number of marriages. In a few years, no doubt, marriage licenses will be sold like dog licenses, good for a period of twelve months, with no law against changing dogs or keeping more than one animal at a time.[16]

My students on the main campus are certainly not prepared to go this far; nor are they the first to think in these terms, which prepare the way for the development Huxley imagined. My own generation deserves that honor and has as its consolation the hard-won knowledge that the wager we made about the meaning and place of sexual intimacy in mortal life, and its bearing on marriage, was often an unsuccessful one.

While it is true that many members of the current generation of students rehearse sentiments that my own generation first believed and defended, there are also healthy signs that they long for a deeper understanding of the bond of marriage than the language of compatibility allows. So long as sexual intimacy is understood to be something peculiarly intimate and personal, however, I do not think that is likely to happen. Biblical writers sought to show the necessary connection between sexual intimacy and marriage; Plato sought to show how erotic love was but a shadow of the philosopher's love of wisdom and, perhaps, a necessary preamble to it. The de-linked condition of the democratic age, however, conspires to make the idea that man is involved in some grander communion largely unthinkable. Exceptions do occur, of course; and anyone who has witnessed a marriage in which, after long years of travail, a man and a woman somehow hover between heaven and earth in the love they demonstrate for one another is not likely to forget it. Such marriages vindicate the institution and give hope that the obstacles that democratic social conditions can present are not the final word. These marriages are, however, rare.

The delinked condition that makes a grander religious or philosophical meaning of sexual intimacy unthinkable, however, also reduces the likelihood that marriage will be thought of as an occasion for reproduction. I have noted in several places that in the democratic age man's time horizon is shortened, so much so that he may come to think that only the present moment matters. This inclines him to think of reproduction as a burden inimical to his immediate desires—which include sexual intimacy, but not the sons and daughters that would issue from it were birth control unavailable. To this should be added that when an adequate basis of marriage is said to be involvement in a "committed relationship," as it often is today, what is presumed is no more than that it is a revocable contract between two disembodied individuals. Reproduction need nowhere be involved.

I do not intend by these comments to suggest that most of my students are thinking this way, but rather that it will be difficult to steer a different course than the one the language and self-understanding they immediately have at their disposal encourages. That is why as these take hold more deeply, population is likely to decline. When Malthus wrote *An Essay on the Principle of Population,* he postulated at the outset that there is "a constant tendency in all animated life to increase beyond the nourishment prepared for it."[17] By this he meant to indicate not simply sexual passion, but also the regeneration of mankind that historically has attended it. As man becomes more delinked, however, the connection between sexual intimacy and reproduction weakens. Malthus presumed that this would not happen. Tocqueville helps us understand why it would.

My students in Qatar increasingly sense themselves to be

disembodied individuals, but the connection between sexual intimacy and reproduction is still largely intact, and marriage is not yet thought of as a "committed relationship," as it often is in America. Indeed, many of my students in Qatar will have their marriages arranged for them. And even if they do not, their choice will be informed by their understanding of the place of their extended family in society. In class one day, I brought to my students' attention the passages from *Democracy in America* in which Tocqueville considers the importance of educating women so that may be able to thoughtfully choose whom they marry. On the main campus, my students generally think these remarks are quaint and outdated. In Qatar, there was an awkward pause and then a question: "Professor Mitchell, do you think our marriages can be happy even if some of us will not be able to fully choose for ourselves?"

It would be rash to conclude that the arranged marriages that make the extended family linkages found in the Middle East possible will soon disappear. In America, Christianity and market commerce militate altogether against the development and maintenance of the extended family; in the Middle East, Islam and the commercial arrangements found there tend to reinforce it. Nevertheless, my students in Qatar confirm that the de-linkage Tocqueville saw in Europe and America has begun to happen in the Middle East as well. I suspect, but cannot prove, that the result will be a very uneven mix between those who retain the understandings they have inherited and those who, finding no middle ground, reject them and turn away from having sons and daughters altogether. However it works out, it is not hard to imagine that the Middle East, too, will soon see population declines of the sort that were thought to be endemic only to the developed world.

The Deeper Crisis

I began the previous section by suggesting that the debt crisis in the developed world is more than an economic crisis. As conditions of equality come to prevail, marriages—should they be wanted at all—will produce ever fewer sons and daughters. Moreover, as I suggested earlier in the chapter, as conditions of equality come to prevail, our sons and daughters will find the idea of failure, so necessary for market commerce to bring about improvement, increasingly unpalatable.

This twin development—which is elicited by delinked, democratic social conditions—has brought us to an impasse that cannot be easily resolved.

In our thinking about the household broadly understood (as economics), we are unprepared to fully account for the payments due and the debt owed, because the failures that would occur if we did are increasingly too terrifying to contemplate. In our thinking about the household narrowly understood (as the family), we are in the process of severing the time-honored link between sexual intimacy and reproduction, and are increasingly unprepared to bear the overwhelming costs, pecuniary and personal, of having and raising the sons and daughters who will amply replace us. Sexual intimacy without the burden of reproduction: a formula by which the current generation proclaims that it owes little or nothing to future generations—that its immediate pleasures are not bound by a larger economy of payment and debt of the sort that is necessarily put in place because we are merely mortal creatures. Such is the accounting system so many of us adhere to today.

I suspect any number of economic proposals and plans will be put forward to address the problem of escalating debt in a world that evinces an increasing imbalance between younger workers and older retirees. I do not think, however, that we will make any real progress unless and until we realize that while the problem we face *manifests* itself today in the domain of economics, its breadth and depth extends beyond what the science of economics can comprehend: we have, in short, lost sight of the inconvenient fact that we live in a world of payment and debt. In the democratic age, we deceive ourselves into thinking that this perennial truth—with which every previous generation has had to contend, and which informed its thinking about economics, family, and even God—has been superseded. Yet the conditions of social equality in the democratic age bid us to do just that.

4 *Religion*

Under Eden's Spell

On the cold winter morning in February 2005 that found me trundling out to the Eastern Shore to investigate those several acres of wetland forest that beckoned, I passed a small church situated not much more than a mile from my final destination. A bit tired from the long drive, but curious about the sorts of denominations I might find in the area, I glanced over at the sign, which read: Antioch Methodist Church. How whimsical our world can be: my mother's family, from Indiana, had been Methodist; and my father's family, from the mountains of Lebanon, was Antioch Orthodox. The liturgical practices of each, I suspected, would have been horrifying to the other. Yet here, not far from what would become my new home, was a church whose name incorporated both halves of my lineage. Unassuming, rebuilt in the early part of the twentieth century after a fire had burned the original nineteenth-century woodframe structure to the ground, the modest building was surrounded by once-majestic oaks and maples now grown old and tired, as if fatigued from being the constant, hovering witness to nearly two centuries of tears shed around the grave sites they overlooked.

On the many subsequent trips I made to the Eastern Shore that winter and spring, I would often wander through the graveyard at the Antioch Methodist Church, in search of clues to lives, short and long, that were put to their final rest under that canopy of oak and maple. In part, it was my way to begin calibrating my new life to the distinct rhythm of the Eastern

Shore; more importantly, it was a way to place the worries of the world in their proper perspective. One gravestone in particular always drew me near:

> *The pains of death are past.*
> *Labor and sorrow cease,*
> *And life's long warfare*
> *Closed at last,*
> *Her soul is found in peace.*

I do not think my students understand Christianity. In Qatar, of course, they can hardly be held responsible for not knowing about a religion that is not their own. In America, on the other hand, many of my students at Georgetown are denominationally Roman Catholic. Some are Protestant. While childhood years spent in pews watching the liturgy or undergoing initiation rites of one sort or another certainly prepare them to recite creedal statements about their faith, few know of "labor and sorrow" or of "life's long warfare." They are still under Eden's spell. They are decades away from the frail thoughts of old age and the betrayal of their bodies, from the breathtaking realization that from dust they come and to dust they go. Under Eden's spell, they cannot know that. Under Eden's spell, they cannot understand Christianity.

The Problem of Evil

When I teach about Christianity in both Qatar and in America, my aspirations are modest. I always begin with what has historically been called the theodicy problem: the problem of evil. It is not a problem with which Christianity alone has to contend. Indeed, it is a problem that is endemic to all monotheisms.

If there are *no* gods, it is impossible to speak of evil, and therefore no way to formulate evil as a problem. If there are no gods, there will be talk of cause and effect in the physical world, and, for us, there will be talk about pleasure and pain—or, to use language befitting the democratic age, about experiences that are "positive" or "negative." Evil, however, will have no referent. When other people are the source of our "negative" experiences, we will likely provide a psychological or sociological account of what has gone wrong; and we will set ourselves to the task of gently or forcibly reforming them by offering the right sort of therapy or the right sort of supports and compensations. Such are the aspirations reflexively adopted by nearly all of us today, even those who call themselves Christians.

If there are *many* gods, it is possible to talk about evil, but properly speaking there is as yet no problem of evil. That is because if there are many gods, some can be good and some can be evil. The explanation for evil then lies in what certain evil gods have done.

If there are only *two* gods—or only two principles, or two substances, as in Zoroastrianism or in Manichaeism—it is possible to talk about evil, but there is still as yet no problem of evil. Here the cosmos is locked in a colossal struggle between good and evil, between light and darkness, or between the spirit and the body; but evil can still be accounted for without difficulty. It comes from one of the two gods, principles, or substances in the cosmos, which are coordinate with one another, if not co-equal.

When I ask my Christian students in America and my Muslim students in Qatar if they believe that good and evil are both equally real, and therefore "substances," almost all of them raise their hands. I congratulate them and tell them whatever their doctrinal professions, they have just declared themselves to be more akin to Zoroastrians or Manichaeans than to monotheists. They are invariably surprised. Monotheism, I tell them, is not something that comes natural to the mortal imagination; that is why in all of its iterations, monotheism has always been beset with heresies.

If there is only *one* God, and if he is Good, then the theodicy problem, the problem of evil, comes into view. It is a formidable one. That is because if God is Good, then he cannot be the cause of evil we witness in the created world. How, then, can we account for evil?

The Christian account is that God created the world *ex nihilo*, literally "out of nothing." The *ex nihilo* claim is a theologically important one, because if God had created the world out of himself, then it would be impossible for there to be any evil whatsoever. If there was, God's substance would be implicated in that evil. If God is Good, however, that cannot be the case. Hence, *creatio ex nihilo*.

The last creature to be created, in the Christian account, was man. God made man in such a way that he, alone in the created world, could willfully defect from God and turn toward darkness. In the book of Genesis, of course, Adam and Eve do just that (Gen. 3:7). They may have been tempted by Satan to do so, but they would not have succumbed had they not been created in such a way that that they could have turned away from God in the first place. Upon theological reflection, this gave rise to the doctrine of the Fall of man, which has been the controversial centerpiece of Christian theology ever since. The evil that occurs in the world is apprehended by this doctrine. Man, not God, brings evil into the world.

The Fall of Man

My students everywhere are perplexed by this doctrine of the Fall of man. Muslims are perplexed because there is no such doctrine in Islam, the reason for which I will mention later. Many Christians in America are perplexed because the doctrine has seemingly become the sole possession of the evangelical community, which is all too often viewed with suspicion and incredulity, and which is said by cosmopolitans to be an archaism not worthy of serious attention. The last great theologian to illuminate and defend the doctrine within the mainline Protestant churches was Reinhold Niebuhr, before and in the aftermath of World War II. By his own admission, he failed to convince the churches of the need to return to orthodoxy. I think this is unfortunate, for it has left the mainline churches without armament. The substance of what is offered there today more properly belongs to modern psychology and sociology than to theology. The laity, for its part, speaks incessantly about "community" but not "church," about God's mercy toward us but not his judgment against the brokenness we display. Reverence and awe have all but disappeared—save for the services run by the children, to which parents are supremely attentive. Convinced not of the brokenness of man but rather of his goodness and innocence, the doctrine of the Fall of man has no place in the mainline churches today, which seem all too content with timely platitudes from the pulpit and green Jell-O salads after the service.

Most of my students understand that the doctrine of the Fall of man pertains to man's sinfulness. Because the term "sin" often brings with it associations that make a fair hearing unlikely, I introduce the notion with the Greek word *hamartia*, which appears in the Greek New Testament wherever we today would read the word "sin." The Greek word *hamartia* literally means "missing the mark." The term is associated with archery, the art of which lends itself well to explaining the phenomenon that the word "sin" names.

Any one of my noble students who has shot an arrow at a target some distance away will have noticed that the force of gravity will always cause him to miss his mark. Adjustments can be made, of course, so that the archer hits his target, but only after a number of comparisons are made between where the archer intended the arrow to go and where it actually does go. Now imagine a situation, I tell my students, where the force of gravity changes after every shot. The adjustment you may have made for the previous shot turns out not to work so well for this next one, and so on. The archer's aim may be true, but he will always miss the mark, no matter how he adjusts. Sin is the curse of the archer whose aim is often good, but who can never hit his target, because each well-intentioned shot he makes operates in a different circumstance than did the previous one.

The Christian claim, I tell my students, is that we are all archers who miss the mark. Always. No amount of learning can eradicate the fundamental problem. It is always already there, in every choice we make, no matter how well-intentioned we may be. It is not a learning problem because the problem is not one of knowledge, but rather of pride, of an always already corrupt will.

We declare our love for God—yet we fall short of the gratitude, humility, and sacrifice that a holy life would entail, and in the end have reason to wonder if we love God or the narrow and self-serving understanding we have of him.

We declare our love for his created world—yet we fall short in our stewardship, and in the end have reason to wonder if we have recklessly exploited our standing at the zenith of creation or hidden behind the pretext of environmentalism, which would make us unwelcome or alien invaders possessed of the self-satisfied knowledge that if we can just stay out of the way, we will remain morally pure.

We declare our love for our country—yet we fall short in our citizenship, and in the end have reason to wonder if our professed longing for liberty is not exceeded by our secret desire to be a docile ward of the state or, better still, to live as if the era of politics and its associated labor has been transcended altogether.

We declare our love for our wives and husbands—yet we fall short, and in the end have reason to wonder if our marriages have been but caricatures of what they might have been, had we put service to them before the ambitions that turned out to provide refuge for our own self-absorption.

We declare our love for our children—yet we fall short of being the fathers and mothers we are called to be, and in the end have reason to wonder if our real intention has been to shape our sons and daughters in our own image, despite our earnest professions to the contrary.

Yes, I tell my students, the Christian claim is that we are archers who miss the mark. Always. That is because our pride obtrudes in all that we do. Pride is, in effect, the gravitational force that causes us all to miss the mark. Like the massive stars in the night sky that bend light around themselves as they go by, man's pride bends the world around himself. We do not need to look into the far reaches of the universe to confirm the wondrous curvature of the universe that Einstein postulated; we have merely to look within, at ourselves.

My students on the main campus and those in Qatar do not struggle to understand what I have said so far. No matter how protected their lives have been, they have lived long enough to have witnessed this pride, this curvature, for themselves—either within themselves or in those they love. With their eyes, they silently confirm that they know what I mean, and seem surprised that they came to class that morning unaware that just this most primal of wounds would be examined that day.

All three monotheisms—Judaism, Christianity, and Islam—acknowledge this wound that does not, by itself, heal. Pride is man's great wound, for which God alone can provide the salve. Man cannot, by himself, heal his wound. Here, too, all three monotheisms agree.

The Incarnation

What distinguishes Christianity from the other two monotheisms is its assessment of how deeply injured man is and what manner of healing is needed as a consequence of the wound he has incurred. The Christian claim is not simply that man's pride bends the world around himself as a massive star bends light around itself; the claim is that so massive is this pride that man is, in effect, a black hole, a universe unto himself, letting no light escape that comes near. That is why Christian writers have often called man's sin a catastrophe. Like a black hole that rips its way through the stars in the night sky, sin wreaks havoc on everything man comes near. Each man is a universe unto himself; cut off from God and the world he damages as he passes through it, he is oblivious to his transgressions and quick to look elsewhere for an explanation of the wreckage that he sees nearby.

I tell my students that the early Christian fathers did not develop this understanding of man's broken nature in isolation, but rather in concert with their developing understanding of the Incarnation. The question that took several centuries to settle, more or less, was whether Christ was divine, merely mortal, or simultaneously both. In the Nicene Creed (AD 381), Christ is said to be simultaneously God and man, and church doctrine has not been altered since. Why, my students ask, is Christ both God and man—why *must* that be the case for Christians?

I do not think many of my students on the main campus understand this doctrine. Like so many students in America, they look to Christ because he is a teacher and an exemplar—hence the popular saying: "What would Jesus do?" He is, in short, a really good man, who teaches us how to be moral, to turn the other cheek, and above all that we should take care of the poor. Many of my students in Qatar, on the other hand, have been taught that Christianity is not monotheistic at all, because it professes three Gods: God the Father, Jesus Christ, and the Holy Spirit. The Christian response to this charge is that God is Triune, having one Being, though with three persons. Understanding the *philosophical* distinction between being (*ousia*) and persons (*hypostasis*) is one thing, however; understanding it from the standpoint of faith is another. Because it is not within my purview or competence to draw them in that direction in class, I turn our attention instead to the misunderstanding many Christians have about Christ—that he is really just a very good man—and to why that does not accord with Christian doctrine.

This misunderstanding is not a recent one from which my students alone suffer. Indeed, the first substantial doctrinal crisis after Emperor Constantine's Edict of Milan (AD 313) legalized Christianity in Rome concerned just this question. Known as the Arian controversy, it was perhaps the greatest doctrinal threat the church has ever faced. Into the heat of this controversy came St. Athanasius, whose little book, *On the Incarnation* (AD 335), it would not be off the mark to say, consolidated the Christian understanding of the simultaneous Divinity and mortality of Christ.

After Adam's turn away from God, Athanasius wrote, the chasm between God and man became unbridgeable. On the occasion of Adam's sin, to put the matter in an odd sort of way, God and man became immiscible. Like oil and water, God and man did not mix. How, then, could communion be restored between God and man; how could oil and water be made to mix?

Athanasius does not recur to this image of the immiscibility of oil and water to describe what the catastrophe of sin wrought, though his argument is well-illuminated by it. It is helpful, I think, because like the image of the archer, it makes the issue at hand quite palpable. Abstract ideas, especially when teaching about religion, are seldom helpful. The immiscibility of oil and water as an image of the relationship between God and man after Adam's sin is something my students on both the main campus and in Qatar can understand quite easily. How, aided by this image, can God and man be brought together?

Athanasius considers three different ways. First, could the angels have done this? They are good, to be sure; but they are spiritual and do not die, and so are not enough like man. They remain on the divine side of the boundary that separates God from man. They are, let us say, oil. Second, could a really good man accomplish this reunification? A really good man, unlike the angels, is mortal and dies, like us; but such a man remains on the mortal side of the boundary and so cannot bring God and man together again. A really good man, no matter how good, is still, let us say, water, just like the rest of us. What remains?

The third way—for Athanasius, the only way—that God and man can be brought together involves the mediation by someone who has a divine nature, like God or his angels, and also a mortal nature, like man. Said otherwise, the third alternative involves the introduction of something both oily and watery that can bring oil and water together in a way that the other alternatives—an angel or a good man—cannot.

My students generally anticipate what follows, for at home and at school they must wash up. The oil that clings to their hands and face must somehow be removed, and they know that water alone is not up to the task. And so they mix in a third thing, namely, soap. In their Chemistry 101 class, I remind them, they learned that a soap molecule has a water-friendly (polar) portion and an oil-friendly (non-polar) portion. A portion of the soap molecule therefore attracts the water and a portion attracts the oil. Neither oil alone nor water alone can bring the other substance toward it; what is needed is a third substance that is simultaneously both. Athanasius wrote that Christ *had* to be both divine and mortal at the same time, or else God and man would have remained immiscible for all time. Christ was therefore "born of a woman," in the words of the Nicene Creed, though also "begotten not made." If he had not been "born of a woman," he would have been merely just another angel; if he had been "made," rather than "begotten," he would have been simply mortal like the rest of us. Christ is the soap molecule, simultaneously oily and watery, simultaneously divine and mortal, the necessary mediator between God and man.

I have raised these matters, of course, not with a view to defending Christianity but rather to explain its two central doctrinal claims: the Fall of man and the necessary mediation of Christ, the Incarnate God/man. I remind my student that these two doctrines require each other. That is, if there is no Fall of man, then there is no need for the Incarnation.

So great is the wound in man that God had to send himself in mortal form in order to bring man back to God: thus says the Christian. Without the wound, without the great transgression against God, it would be senseless to talk about the Incarnation at all. That is why the New Testament is called the Gospel—the Good News. Without it, the great transgression could not have been healed and the unbridgeable gap between God and man would have remained in place. Without it, man's lot, in short, would have remained forever under the shadow of the bad news of death and suffering, which were the burdens laid upon him for his original transgression against God.

On the main campus, these reflections give my purportedly Christian students an opportunity to rethink their Arianism, be it implicit or explicit. In Qatar, these reflections give my Muslim students an opportunity to distinguish more clearly between Islam and Christianity. In Islam, interestingly enough, there is no book of Genesis, as there is for both Jews and Christians. This is not to say that there is no account of Creation or of the Garden of Eden and man's eviction from it. The Qur'an does, indeed, have such accounts, but they are located throughout, in accordance with a different logic. There, Adam's transgression, so central to the Christian account, does not establish an unbridgeable chasm between God and man; rather, in the Qur'an, the disobedience of Adam is seen as an occasion for shame rather than for catastrophic sin. And, as I have said, if there is no Fall of man, then there is no need for the Incarnation. That is part of the reason why my Muslim students have difficulties understanding Christianity. The wound for which the Incarnation is a salve simply does not exist. No less can be said of Judaism, though of course Judaism and Islam differ on a wide range of other issues.

The Meaning of Suffering

There is, then, a substantial, indeed irreconcilable, doctrinal difference between Christianity and Islam on the matter of the

Fall of man and the Incarnation. I do not remember a single occasion, however, when this was a cause of tension in the classroom in Qatar, or even outside of it. I was, as I mentioned earlier, a guest of gracious hosts. My students knew that my family was Christian on both my father's and mother's side. Our conversations about religion were never grave but always earnest, as they should be.

The biggest squabbles I had with my students, interestingly, were not about the doctrinal differences between Christianity and Islam at all, but rather about suffering—how to respond to it, what it is, and why it happens. In this respect, my students in Qatar were similar to my students on the main campus: neither group really gave enough thought to understanding suffering in terms of their professed religion. My students in Qatar may have *believed* in their own religion more deeply, but that did not make their account of suffering any less formulaic than what most of my students on the main campus believed. In both cases, what was offered was learned rather than earned, so to speak.

Anyone who has suffered or witnessed the suffering of his friends knows to remain silent, knows that no words can at first comprehend it. When, in the Hebrew Bible, Job suffers his horrible affliction, we are told that his friends converge, sit with him on the ground for seven days and nights, and say nothing (Job 2:13). Therein lies wisdom.

Eventually, words *are* necessary. If those words are religiously informed, they must verge more on consolation than on explanation. The man who rushes into the quiet stillness of suffering with a self-assured explanation does not understand the world in which he lives. Perhaps that is the problem with the accounts my students give of suffering: too young to begin to surmise what is in store for them, they think they will not be stricken. Their words come too easily, for they are still under Eden's spell.

What, then, are the consolations that can be offered by friends after patient waiting? Christianity, I tell my students, offers three sorts of consolations. I am certain that Islam offers two of these; Christianity, because it is a *historical* religion forever indebted to Judaism, also offers a third.

The first is to be found in the book of Job, which I have already introduced. The book of Job is perhaps the most inscrutable—even frightening—book of the Hebrew Bible. Near its end, after Job has shown himself to have worshiped God *because he is God* rather than because of the good things that God granted to him on earth, he is given the opportunity to ask God why he suffered as he did. It is a question I suspect all of us would ask if given the chance. God replies: "Where were you when I laid the foundations of the Earth?" (Job 38:4). This is not a direct answer to Job's question, but it is an answer nevertheless: here God tells Job that man's understanding is so meager and deficient that God's inscrutable justice will always escape him. That is why the book of Job is so frightening: man prides himself that he can understand God's justice. He cannot. God is God; man is man. The mortal task is not to understand the inscrutable justice of God but to worship him, to be thankful that man has been given life and breath at all, no matter what he endures here below. The real alternative, the one to which the religious man is ever attentive, is never to have been born at all.

When I look out at my young students in class, I often wonder who among them will display this kind of gratitude when overwhelmed by suffering, who among them will have faith strong enough to declare that their suffering, too, is a testimony to God's glory?

The second consolation offered by Christianity for suffering is that it deepens the soul. God's justice is inscrutable here, but not his mercy, which carries the man of faith beyond what he can, by himself, bear; and in time yields the gifts of patience, humility, and wisdom. We need not take this path, of course. The other, easier path requires only that we declare that there are no hidden lessons to be learned from what has just happened; and that we walk on alone, without the gnawing sense that God is speaking directly to us through adversity. When Job's wife declared to him that he should "curse God and die" (Job 2:9) after he was afflicted, she was giving voice to just this sentiment. Suffering has no purpose. Life is wretched. That is all.

To the man of faith, however, that is not all—much to the incredulity of the worldly-wise. The suffering man of faith intimates that just this lot is his; and knows that he is called at once to conform to it, yet to rise above it. Dwelling in that paradox, the man of faith abides both in the event that has befallen him and in the subterranean place where his heart has settled and his conscience listens. "The fire that burns the chaff purifies the gold," Augustine says in his *City of God*. "Though the suffering be the same, the sufferer is different."[1] Most of my students are too young to have been exposed to suffering of the sort that can deepen them, should they be drawn onward by faith's consolation. They have taken notes in class diligently for a dozen years or more. The four greatest teachers—friendship, love, suffering, and death—have not yet tested their pupils, however, or conveyed their lessons.

The third consolation offered by Christianity for suffering is that it is not the final word. God's justice is inscrutable here, too; but not his promise. Christianity, I tell my students, is a historical religion. By this I do not mean, simply, that it *has* a history; rather, that Christianity comprehends history as a fulfillment of God's promise. Each moment in time, therefore, always points beyond itself, to a fulfillment that God foreknew from all Eternity, and which man can only dimly see, through the eyes of faith.

The awesome origin of this understanding is not to be found in Christianity, however, but rather in Judaism. It was the ancient Hebrews who upended the archaic, cyclical formula: all that is novel is death and error; in repetition alone is there comfort. Through the witness of the Hebrews, we hear for the first time that history moves toward redemption and, therefore, that *every* evil that befalls the Jewish people, from the Egyptian captivity to—God have mercy—the Holocaust, is supervened by God's promise to deliver them out of the lion's den (Dan. 6:16) and into the land of milk and honey (Exod. 33:3), though not yet. Every historical event is now more than it appears to be, its terror no less than its triumph attenuated and recalibrated.

Where Jews await the promised Messiah, Christians claim he has already arrived; and not only for the redemption of the body Israel, but for the whole world. Yet the Christian claim is not that the already-present Messiah has put an end to history, but rather that historical existence now has a twofold character: at once broken because of Adam's sin; at once redeemed because of Jesus the promised Messiah's sacrifice.

Niebuhr argued that the deepest justification for democratic government of the sort the United States has had rests on just this twofold historical fact: because man is broken and not to be trusted, periodic elections, a vigilant press, the legal protection of rights, and checks and balances between the three branches of government are necessary; because man is redeemed, the rule of law, a federal government with limited enumerated powers, and a polity infused with the spirit of liberty are possible. This twofold historical fact had implications for foreign policy as well: mindful that man is broken, we must proceed with the understanding that nations act, sometimes brutally, in their own self-interest; mindful that man is redeemed, we must not lose hope that someday cooperation between nations will make a peaceful world possible—though not yet.

Hope

Hope, in fact, must be the watchword for the Christian who seeks consolation in the broken world in which he dwells. This is not the superficial hope that sometimes goes under the name of "optimism." Optimism is gleeful; the man who would orient himself by it takes the current bright and shining moment as the measure—and then falls off into pessimism when the darkness of subsequent events invades and overwhelms him, as it must. Optimism and pessimism, like manic depression, are opposite sides of the same coin; hope is another currency altogether, more precious than gold. Hope is steadfast; it maintains its hold when every event is understood to be but a foreshadowing of God's providential plan.

Most of my students on the main campus do not yet understand hope. Many of them live largely from moment to moment and alternate between cheery optimism and brooding pessimism. To be young is to suffer from this affliction; to live in the democratic age is to find few antidotes to alleviate it. The relentless pace of life blurs or severs the connection between past, present, and future. In such circumstances, living in the moment is often all that seems possible for the young, and increasingly for the old too. Forgetting the past, isolated in the present, oriented by a future they intimate should provide a reprieve from their current benumbed condition, many of my students openly dream of "change." Only nominally Christian, they dwell in the shadow of their religion and not in its light: steady hope has yielded to the oscillation of optimism and pessimism; and faith in God's providential history has given way to an ill-defined need for change. Feasting nearly out of sight of a religion they do not really understand, I wonder how much nourishment they really derive from the moods that alternatingly overtake them and the ideas that they say they believe.

The relentless pace of life in the democratic age is not the final word, however. The retrospective gaze granted by each passing year sometimes reveals in microcosmic form what Christianity declares about the wondrous arc of history itself—namely, that events are always more than they first appear to be. I tell my students that I remember with crystal clarity the humid first morning after my family arrived in Ann Arbor on a summer evening in 1963. From across the street came a freckle-faced, redheaded, scrawny little eight-year-old, with his loyal dog Sharpy, which I soon learned none of his other friends could stand, but which he defended in his inimitable, mad, Irish-tempered way. He quickly became my best friend.

He was an extraordinary musician, and during the upheaval of the 1960s we would gather around the piano at his house and at mine for hours, working out three- or four-part harmonies, *a cappella*, with our other dear friends, which we sang shuffling through the autumn leaves, the dry winter snows, and the soggy spring days of the school year. Forty years later he would die of cancer, surrounded, still, by friends from Ann Arbor and from other places, who sat like Job's friends, patiently waiting. After all that we had been through during those intervening decades, who among us, at the end, could have guessed how life was to unfold on that humid summer morning in 1963? Yet not one of us who has been left behind was surprised, in retrospect, by all that happened.

The events of life are always more than they first appear to be, and only fully perspicuous from God's eternal vantage. Hope recognizes this and puts an end to the flattering illusion that we can ever definitively comprehend ourselves or the world in which we dwell. In the democratic age, everything is in motion; and in our mad rush to understand what little of it we can, we either oversimplify what we witness or declare it to be a jumble that has no coherence whatsoever. Yet when suffering obtrudes, hope reminds us that our world is more wondrous than we can possibly imagine. Too young, really, for this sort of reverence, many of my students—even those who would count themselves among the religious—are drawn to accounts of suffering that are less mysterious and whose lineaments are purportedly easier to trace. They generally find what they think they are looking for in psychological or sociological accounts—both of which purport to identify and eliminate the suffering that overtakes man, though without reference to God, to evil, or to a fault that lies, always already, in everyone.

I am not surprised by this, really. Tocqueville thought that in the democratic age the abiding concern for well-being would overpower the soul, make man attentive almost exclusively to the material world and to the scientific explanations that presuppose its preeminence. He would, consequently, come to believe that suffering can be altogether eliminated. In such a world, God can be more easily forgotten. The disposition of my students to account for suffering in non-religious idioms corroborates the developments that Tocqueville predicted. I remain unconvinced, however, that these accounts are, finally, adequate to the suffering that man endures. Its ache is too deep and its origin too remote from what any science of man can disclose.

Growing up in Ann Arbor, I had read the Twenty-Third Psalm on any number of occasions, but I first *heard* it at age forty-eight, as I read it aloud standing at the foot of my best friend's hospital bed: "The Lord is my shepherd; I shall not want." Only when man's world has been upended by suffering, and the long-standing consolations of mortal life have been torn from him, can he perhaps begin to understand that God's enveloping love is all that remains. Until then, he remains deaf, and any effort to convince him otherwise will be in vain. Yet there, in that moment, he discovers hope.

The Permanence of Religion

I have not been particularly careful here to distinguish between the sentiments of my students on the main campus and my students in Qatar. Because they are all young, neither group thinks deeply about suffering. When prompted, however, my Christian students on the main campus are disposed to first think about it in psychological or sociological terms; only when reminded of their Christian inheritance do they strain to think about suffering in religious terms. Many of my Muslim students in Qatar, on the other hand, are disposed to think about suffering in religious terms first and then, thanks to the increasing prominence of the social sciences in the universities in the Middle East, ponder whether psychology and sociology offer a better account. While I cannot prove it, I suspect that these latter sorts of explanations will increasingly take hold of the imagination, at least among the university educated. For both my main campus and Qatar students, no matter what their religion, there is bound to be a great deal of confusion. The thoughts and sentiments that come naturally to the democratic imagination, Tocqueville wrote, often conflict with long-standing religious understandings. No religion will survive unaltered, though some will be altered more than others.

It is worth stating clearly here that Tocqueville did not think that religion would disappear in the democratic age. On the contrary, he thought that religion was a permanent facet of mortal life, no less so for us than for our ancestors. The living shape of religion may change, but it cannot die. My students in Qatar certainly wonder about the substance of Christian belief in America; but their deeper perplexity pertains to the blunt fact that America, the most modern country in the world, is also one of the most religious. How is this possible, they wonder. To be modern—doesn't this necessarily involve the renunciation of religious belief? This was certainly the prejudice of European intellectuals and their heirs elsewhere. Tocqueville did not share it:

> The philosophers of the eighteenth century explained the gradual weakening of beliefs in an altogether simple fashion. Religious zeal, they said, will be extinguished as freedom and enlightenment increase. It is unfortunate that the facts do not accord with this theory.[2]

Tocqueville thought that the interesting question was not whether religion would wither away in the democratic age, but rather why it had temporarily fallen into disrepute in Europe. The brief answer was that the Roman Catholic Church in Europe had aligned itself with the extant political powers during the aristocratic age. When those powers were over-thrown, the Roman Catholic Church was severely weakened as well. Guilt by association explained the European anomaly. Secularization was the exception, not the rule.

In America, on the other hand, an uneven but workable separation of religion and politics had made it possible for each to thrive. Religion may have been "the first of their po-litical institutions,"[3] as Tocqueville put it; but religion ruled only *indirectly*, by shaping habits and character so that citizens could bear the burdens of liberty. Not in the voting booth, but in the pews was liberty ultimately vouchsafed. Not only *could* religion and political liberty work harmoniously together in the democratic age; they must do so.

In the Middle East, it is well to remember, European colo-nization occurred *after* the churches had lost much of their sway in Europe, *after* the conclusion had been reached that to be modern is to cast religion aside. The period of colonial rule in the Middle East saw Europeans, and even indigenous rul-ers, attempt to instantiate this understanding in law, adminis-tration, and culture. Although colonial rule ended long ago, its traces still remain. For many of my students in Qatar, an agonizing choice confronts them: be religious or be modern. Most Americans do not understand this. I tell my students in Qatar that the either/or choice they think they need to make is a legacy of European colonization; and that America, not Eu-rope, is where they should look if they want to understand that religion can have a place today and in the future.

When Religion Is a "Way of Life"

Tocqueville may have thought that religion was eternal in man, but he thought that Islam, or at least a certain rendition of it, was not likely to thrive in the democratic age.[4] I tell my students that while he singles out Islam in *Democracy in Amer-ica*, Tocqueville's deeper concern was with religious ortho-doxy. So understood, his apprehension could equally apply to the theonomists within Christianity. (Orthodox Judaism is a more complicated matter, because the pages of the Torah juxtapose both Law and rabbinic commentary.)

The issue with which Tocqueville was concerned, if I may so put it, is whether religion is understood to be a comprehensive doctrine—a "way of life." One of the reasons Tocqueville thought Christianity would thrive in the democratic age was that it offered only general precepts about man's relationship to God and to his neighbors. Christianity offered no cosmology; no comprehensive body of law; no plan for the adjudication of conflict; no express theory of politics, economics, or ethics; no set rules about the institution of marriage; no guidelines about how children are to be raised; no schedule of daily prayer; no dietary restrictions; no specifications for the inheritance of land; no list of tasks a believer must accomplish before he dies; no incontrovertible account of how Christ's atoning sacrifice is to be made present in creation after his ascension; and on and on. Christianity, in other words, is not a comprehensive whole; a great many matters are left outside of its purview.

To be sure, the Christian churches did develop any number of understandings about these and other matters, and often defended them with alacrity. It is well to remember, however, that Christianity emerged against the backdrop of Hebrew, Greek, and Roman civilizations. The laws, traditions, and conventions that these civilizations had already put in place were seldom eliminated completely; sometimes they were modified but often simply left in place. By virtue of when and where it arrived on the world historical stage, Christianity was unlikely to become a comprehensive doctrine. Even when it tried to develop its own understandings, it could not do so without borrowing ideas from these three civilizations that never quite exactly comported with its own.

Orthodoxies, on the other hand, purport to offer a comprehensive doctrine, a complete way of life. The phrase "way of life" is a relatively recent one. When it is invoked, it is generally understood to be a counterpoint to the disjointed condition of the democratic age and a promise of a religious resolution to that condition—not in the future, when God returns in judgment, or in the afterlife, but rather *now*.

I tell my students that Tocqueville thought that the disjointed condition of the democratic age could not be eliminated. Indeed, he thought it a mark of moral integrity to be able to live in this disjointed age without looking back in a melancholic way to an enchanted past or with delight to some future post-revolutionary moment. Religious orthodoxy holds out against our disjointed condition, in some measure flirting with re-enchantment or with the revolutionary urge to put an end to the current state of things, or with both. If religion teaches us how to live *in* this disjointed democratic age, Tocqueville thought it a blessing; if religion teaches us to flee *from* that condition, he thought there would be no end to our troubles.

That is why Tocqueville thought it significant that Christianity proffered only general ideas about the relationship between God and man and between man and man. The two great Commandments "Thou shalt love the Lord thy God with all thy heart, and with all thy soul, and with all thy mind" and "Thou shalt love thy neighbor as thyself" (Matt. 22:37, 39) are binding; but they can accommodate new developments in science, law, politics, economics, family structure, public health, and nutrition. In the democratic age, everything moves; a religion that does not place man in that flow of ever-changing events while at the same time giving him hope and encouragement will be at odds with the spirit of the age. Christianity, Tocqueville thought, can do that.

Democratic Modifications of Religion in America

Religion may be eternal to man, and Christianity may have certain advantages over religious orthodoxy in the democratic age, but no religion will remain unmodified by the condition of equality that characterizes that age. Remarkable changes have in fact already occurred within Christianity, to which many of my students on the main campus bear witness. The sentiments of many of my Muslim students in Qatar suggest that similar changes are occurring within Islam as well.

It is well to remember that what is at issue in the democratic age is the condition of and prospect for delinked man, who emerges when the social hierarchy of the aristocratic age collapses and "each man is thrown back on himself," as Tocqueville put it. Believing in equality yet never really sure of his standing, always rushing around because of the competition of all against all, never able to patiently dwell in the formalities of life, democratic man will want his religion to be straightforward and clear in its meaning, doctrines, and requirements. Because he is also suspicious of the claim that any other man has a more privileged position than he does, he will insist upon a direct and unmediated connection to God. Finally, because democratic man does not want to believe that anything exceeds his grasp, he will bring God down to his own level. When I tell my main campus students these things, they do not want to believe that much of what they have been exposed to in their churches is a predictable result of just these democratic developments.

When they go to church, my students often hear some variant of the doctrine of universal salvation—but seldom wonder whether it is advocated and embraced because of the democratic prejudice that everyone is equal, and therefore that no one should be barred from the gates of Heaven. I remind them that if that is true, man can do whatever he thinks he wants to do here below and still be assured of a place in the Everlasting Kingdom, and that the long-standing conviction that life is a trial loses all meaning if that is so.

When they go to church, students occasionally hear that God wants them to have worldly success—but seldom wonder if that claim is best understood in light of the middle-class anxiety that the age of democracy produces. When no one is

assured of their place in society, when each man has enough
to taste of the blessings of prosperity but not enough to be assured that he cannot lose what he has, material life becomes
a source of never-ending anxiety. Would not one of the blessings of God, who loves man, be his assurance that if man loves
God, he will be blessed with material abundance? Ever fixed
on the material world, democratic man wishes to bargain
with God about the blessings he bestows. America: a nation
of traders. Augustine and the other early church fathers would
be horrified.

When they go to church, my students witness an increasingly stripped-down liturgy, which is both shorter and more
informal than it was even a generation ago. Always in a hurry,
democratic man does not have time for formalities; he wants
the *Cliffs Notes* version of reality from his religion and from everything else. He wants the clear and simple truth of religion
immediately exposed by the full light of day and wonders why
the rituals of the church are necessary at all.

From what was once the church choir, my students may still
hear hymns, but a grand several-century tradition of church
music in America is nearing an end; parishioners scarcely
know the melodies and are generally inattentive to the words
that would at least serve as a counterpoint to what passes for
the sermon they hear. In its stead, parishioners increasingly
hear electric guitars accompanying songs whose structure and
melody are more akin to pop music, complete with a lyrical
"hook" of the sort my band's musical agent so long ago kept
telling us to include in the country music songs we wrote.

In those churches that place the Bible on the altar, my students hear sermons that exposit the Word of God, literally
understood—but seldom wonder if there is a reason why biblical "literalism" emerges in the democratic age and not before.
Far from being anathema to the spirit of the democratic age, I
tell my students that biblical literalism is almost inevitable. It is
a small step from the suspicion of ornate and symbolic liturgy
to a suspicion of reading the Bible allegorically, symbolically,

mythically. Absent time and training, the wonders that such readings reveal cannot emerge. Democratic man seldom has patience or interest enough. During the Scopes "monkey trial" of 1925 in Tennessee, a literal interpretation of the account of Creation found in the book of Genesis was juxtaposed against the modern scientific account of evolution. Both biblical literalism and modern science, however, demand the same thing: clear and simple truth. So understood, what was demonstrated by the Scopes trial was *not* the incompatibility of Christianity and modern science, but rather the inappropriateness of using interpretive criteria that emerge in the democratic age to understand the Bible itself, or at least to use them by themselves. What was really on trial was biblical literalism, not Christianity. At the end of his *Confessions*, written in 398, Augustine offered a non-literal reading of the book of Genesis. I suspect that it is compatible with the conclusions of modern science. It never would have occurred to him to expect the Bible to be clear and simple. Only democratic man seeks that.

When they are in church, my students largely take for granted that they, not their pastors or priests, hold the keys to Heaven — but seldom wonder whether this idea, too, emerges not coincidentally in the democratic age. The idea that a priest whose authority has been handed down through apostolic succession might bar them from the gates of Heaven strikes them as strange and unwarranted. They take for granted that pastors and priests are for counsel and guidance, and that their own relationship to God is a direct one, unmediated by the church and its appointed mediaries. They are generally surprised to learn that this issue divided Christendom at the dawn of the Reformation period. Many of my Roman Catholic students on the main campus know of the doctrine *Extra Ecclesiam nulla salus*: "Outside the Church there is no salvation." Only a few adhere to the more stringent pre–Vatican II understanding of the doctrine; most of my other Roman Catholic students, are, in this respect, Protestant without knowing it.

When they are in church, my students often hear their

church being referred to as a "community"—but seldom wonder whether renaming the church in this way betrays the deep ambivalence democratic man has toward well-defined institutions with set missions. (That students also hear their own university being referred to as a "community" gives them pause.) A "community" is ill-defined and abstract; yet into it may be poured yearnings that outstrip the specified tasks of the church. Tocqueville noted that in the democratic age the belief in the indefinite perfectibility of man would come to prevail. Convinced that what he has inherited in the way of institutional understandings and liturgical practices can be improved, calling his church a "community" liberates him from the strictures that would otherwise stand in his way.

In those rapidly growing churches that call themselves Charismatic, my students witness services purportedly inspired by the Holy Spirit, which "bloweth where it listeth" (John 3:8). The emphasis on the "gifts of the spirit" announces that a burdensome and ordinary life shaped by the competition of all against all need not be our lot. Indeed, with the "gifts of the spirit," every man may discover how he is extraordinary. In the democratic age, Tocqueville wrote, when each man comes to resemble every other,

> a multitude of artificial and arbitrary classifications are created, with the aid of which each seeks to set himself apart, out of fear of being carried away into the crowd despite himself.[5]

I remind my students that Tocqueville thought that the democratic age would bring social equality to the entire world. If man's pride to distinguish himself is not exceeded by his envy to pull others down to his level, then we can expect to see an increased emphasis on the "gifts of the spirit" within the churches as the world more fully enters the democratic age. That Charismatic Christianity is now the fastest-growing denomination on the planet—that this form of Christianity proclaims a way for each man to be extraordinary at just

the moment he loses himself in the vast sea of humanity—
is suggestive of the pace and extent of the development that
Tocqueville traced.

From the pulpit, my students hear of a God who is not as
distant from man as he was once portrayed to be—but they
seldom wonder if this purported proximity, too, is an artifact
of the democratic age. Aside from imagining his own death,
nothing more frightens democratic man than that his world,
or parts of it, cannot be understood by extending to new
provinces what he already knows with assurance. Parsimony
and the belief in the unity of all knowledge guide his efforts;
with the right amount of courtship, his beloved will come to
see that he is worthy, just as he is. When it comes to religion,
however, this habit of thought runs headlong into the great division at the heart of all monotheisms—between God the Cre-
ator and the world he creates. "Bothered," as Tocqueville put
it, by this primordial division, democratic man is inclined to
blur or erase it altogether.[6] Rather than accept the "otherness"
of God, democratic man renders God in terms familiar to himself. In such capable hands, religion becomes a species of hu-
manism. The tone and substance of worship thereby change:
gone are somberness, sobriety, and reverence; the chasm between God and man is bridged not by the Jesus who mercifully intercedes for our catastrophic sin, but by the Jesus "who
is my friend." Regal language is supplanted, and church attire need be no different from that worn to the shopping mall.
Once man was small and God loomed large, so that man, by
divine imputation, might be made larger than he was; now
man is large and God is small, so that man need no longer be
troubled by his once-diminished stature.

In their churches and outside of them, my students often
hear or utter the phrase "I am spiritual, not religious"—but seldom wonder if this sort of juxtaposition really becomes thinkable only in the democratic age. To be religious is to be bound,
as the Latin word *religio* suggests. In Rome, prior to the advent
of Christianity, the term referred to ancestral veneration and

to the cultivation of practices that appertained to such veneration. In its colloquial use today as a descriptor of Christianity, Judaism, and Islam, religion pertains to a body of beliefs and practices concerning God, his promises to man, and man's debt to him. So understood, religion binds man in one way and not another—this religion, to these beliefs and practices; that religion, to others. Democratic man looks at this religion and that, and doubts that any one of them can be true. Convinced that truth must be "inclusive," he aspires to something more comprehensive than religion, which grasps the genus of which religions are but a species. Hovering over the world, but never quite in it, democratic man arrives at "spirituality," which he takes to be the true ground of a global ecumenism. Here the Christian aspiration for universality has turned on Christian religion itself, which is found to be wanting, mired in archaisms, and not able to provide that ecumenical unity democratic man seeks—or, rather, needs. Spirituality, the argument goes, is superior to Christianity; indeed it is superior to Judaism and Islam as well and is the only basis for abiding concord among all of their respective adherents. Shorn of all encumbrances, democratic man rises gloriously above the seemingly limited incarnations of truth that any one religion proffers, and finds satisfaction less, I suspect, in the universal spirituality he affirms than in superseding the religion he has left behind. The alpha and the omega of "I am spiritual, not religious" is the rejection of the experience of limitation, which the delinked man of the democratic age feverishly desires to overcome, in religion and in everything else. Tocqueville worried that for a time he might actually succeed.

Islam in the Democratic Age

Are there similar developments happening within Islam as well? Of the modifications to Christianity wrought by the conditions of equality in the democratic age, some appear to be making inroads into Islam, while others either have no corresponding referent or are not occurring. The literature on this question is vast, I suspect; my frame of reference here is what I have discerned from my students.

The doctrine of universal salvation has not captured the imagination of my students in Qatar. Like Christianity, Islam claims to offer salvation to all who withstand the trials of mortal life. It does not occur to my students, however, that Islam should hold out the promise that everyone goes through the gates of Heaven, irrespective of what they have done. In a still largely hierarchical society, they understand themselves to be vastly different from one another, and so the thought that they should all share the same fate after death does not immediately occur to them.

Neither are my students in Qatar prone to believe that God shows his love for man by offering him worldly success. When the world is in constant motion and worldly success ill-assured, as it is in America, the thought comes to mind that God's grace is like a lottery, which can at any moment change a man's place in society. In much of the Middle East, the social world is largely fixed: Those who have wealth tend to retain it; those without it rarely envision a radical change in their fortunes, though I suspect this will not be the case into the indefinite future. God is not man's partner in the enterprise of upward mobility, as he often is in America.

Other comparisons are more difficult. For Christians, much of the liturgy *points to* God's mysterious Incarnation and to his promise of redemption. To be sure, portions of the liturgy purport to be the very words uttered by God the Son, and therefore cannot be altered. With respect to the other portions, however, the manner of pointing to that mystery has varied from one church to another and has been altered over the centuries. For Muslims, on the other hand, the Qur'an itself was God's last and final presence in history, which was not only disclosed *in* Arabic, but was constitutive *of* the Arabic language itself. There are, to be sure, large issues that would have to be raised should the Qur'an be subject to what academics call "the historical-critical method"—something that was done to the Bible in the last several centuries within the Protestant and Roman Catholic Churches, and which irrevocably altered each of them. These issues cannot be considered here. For Muslims, the Arabic utterances within a service are not words *about* God that conceivably could be modified without reproach, but rather *God-Words*, if that phrase can be used, which cannot be altered, as much of the Christian liturgy can be. The Qur'an is not the equivalent of the Bible for Christians; it is more akin to Christ himself—the very presence of God in the world. The liturgy within the Christian churches can, within reason, change; within Islam, it cannot.

The matter of the supersession of the traditional mission of the mosque through the invocation of the word "community" is more difficult to parse. Christianity, I remind my students, is not a comprehensive way of life. Its churches are called to act in the name of faith, hope, and charity. While other provinces—commerce, family, politics, and so on—are informed by Christianity, the churches do not have express authority over them. Moreover, by virtue of not being a way of life, Christianity cannot be comprehensive enough to oppose all or even most of the developments in the democratic age. Indeed, identifying a church as a "community" is confirmation that, from the vantage of impatient democratic man, the church has not kept up with the times.

Islam, on the other hand, *does* profess to be a comprehensive way of life. The provinces of commerce, family, politics, and more are within its purview. Islam purports to be *the* inexhaustible whole that no development in history can render limited or obsolete. Thus, democratic impatience with what Islam provides would seem to be impossible, because it is without the sorts of limits that democratic man sees in his church, and which induces him to rename it a "community" in the first place.

The matter is made more complicated because the Islamic term *Umma* means "community." It would seem, then, that the sort of development happening in the Christian churches of America could not occur to Islam in the Middle East. In America, however, Islamic communities are, in fact, appearing everywhere. I do not think this is occurring only because *Umma* can be translated as "community." While I cannot prove it, I suspect that in America the same sort of thing is happening to Islam as has happened to Christianity and to Judaism, namely, that its adherents come to believe that its inherited form is anachronistic, that it must be modified in accordance with the understandings and aspirations of the democratic age—that as a religion it does not quite go far enough, that it is not comprehensive after all, or, rather, not comprehensive in the right way for the democratic age.

For a religion that claims to be comprehensive, this is a remarkable development. It is already well under way for many Protestants and Roman Catholics in America. So, too, is this occurring for Reform Jews in America. There are Protestant communities, Roman Catholic communities, and Jewish Reform communities in great numbers. Muslims will not be far behind. No religion in America is immune to this modification. The delinked condition drives it forward. If this modification begins to occur in the Middle East, if mosques become Islamic communities in the sense that is meant by the term in America, then we will know that the delinked condition has begun to alter the workings of the heart and mind in the region.

The global ecumenism movement that brings Christians, Muslims, and Jews together on the main campus for "interreligious dialogue" has not really captured the imagination of my students in Qatar. They are respectful when colloquia are set up for such dialogue, as Georgetown is wont to do; but I think it safe to say that they are generally much more confident in their religion than Christians on the main campus are of theirs. Students in America learn early on that their religious beliefs are worthy less because they are true than because they are their own. While they will seldom be told they are wrong for believing what they do, they will never be asked whether their religion—or anybody else's—is true. In the democratic age, each man is on his own, with only the dim light of personal experience to guide him on his way. That can never lead him to a truth grander than his own. Instead, in this dimly lit world, he is satisfied if "tolerance" and "diversity" are maintained. These allow each man to continue being a light unto himself, undisturbed, living the life of an Arcadian shepherd.

In Qatar, on the other hand, "tolerance" and "diversity" are not the watchwords they are in America. Most of my students there believe without embarrassment that Islam is true. That they themselves happen to hold this belief has no bearing on the matter. That is why our class discussions were so wonderfully frank and refreshing. A respectful tone always prevailed, but the laborious and delicate task of figuring out how each student's (merely) personal opinion about religion could be tolerated, respected—or, better still, "honored" and "affirmed"—was mercifully absent.

The democratic age privileges recognition, not truth; that is why such a high premium is placed on "tolerance and diversity. And that is also why in the democratic age, inter-religious dialogue will have the prominent place that it does. When inter-religious dialogue is urgently fixed upon in the Middle East, when global ecumenism becomes a looming concern there, then we will know that the delinked condition has begun to alter the workings of the heart and mind in the region.

My students in Qatar are somewhat perplexed when they hear American students say, "I am spiritual, not religious." Several of my students gave me reason to suspect that they did not believe in God at all, but they never said so directly. None of them characterized themselves as "spiritual," however. In America, restlessness and agitation forever prompt the imagination to wonder where rest and repose may be finally found. Not finding it in the external world, where everything seems to be in flux, democratic man looks within. Because each man is equal to every other and has no special claim to knowledge, the repose he seeks must be devoid of contestable content. "Spirituality" provides him with just what he is looking for. It is "inclusive," requires no great sacrifice or effort, and does not bear directly on the everyday tasks of life, except perhaps to take the edge off their harshness.

In the Middle East, on the other hand, Islam purports to speak to nearly every aspect of life. To repudiate Islam does not allow man to carry on, undisturbed, in the external affairs of his life, with just the religious aspect of it modified. Accustomed to thinking that life should be a comprehensive whole, the choice for my students appears to be between Islam or godlessness, and not between being religious or spiritual. The latter presumes that man's internal and external world can be severed. My students who believe that religion is a comprehensive whole cannot accede to that. Should that change, should my Muslim students, like so many of my Christian students in America, start thinking of themselves as "spiritual, not religious," then we will know that the delinked condition has begun to alter the workings of the heart and mind in the region. In America, this development within Islam has already begun. Tocqueville would not have been surprised.

As I have already mentioned, my Muslim students in Qatar take for granted that the Qur'an is God's Arabic Revelation, Word for Word. For many of my students on the main campus, therefore, it is tempting to think that these Muslim students are analogous to the sorts of Christians who are biblical literalists. The term "fundamentalism" dates to the 1917 publication of *The Fundamentals*, a two-volume attempt to wrest American Protestantism back from the theologically liberal arms into which it had fallen. It now serves as a proxy for those who are politically conservative and who derive their conservatism from a literal interpretation of their religious books. Because it is inevitable that our first attempt to understand something new involves extending what we already know from one domain into another, it should not be surprising that many Americans now apply the term both to certain Protestants and to certain Muslims. The use of this term in the Islamic world is not particularly helpful, however. It is less a description of an objective phenomenon than a clinical assessment of a diseased condition, the cure for which is taken to be enlightenment, broadly understood. That is the remedy often offered for fundamentalism in America; so, too, it is proffered for the fundamentalism in the Middle East.

I have already mentioned that for Muslims, the Qur'an is not akin to the Christian Bible. Rather, it is akin to Christ's Incarnation. That is, it is taken to be the irruption of God himself into history. Thus, to call Muslims "fundamentalists" is akin to calling anyone who believes in Christ a "fundamentalist." Doing so misunderstands the important analogy between Christ and the Qur'an.

The invocation of the specter of fundamentalism, then, deflects but does not grasp the deeper problem that has emerged within the Muslim world. By virtue of being a juridical religion, the greatest defenders and illuminators of Islam have always been its jurists. The crisis within the Islamic world begins and ends with them. Few of my students, in Washington or in Qatar, know of the grand and integrative juridical tradition within Islam, which began crumbling centuries ago. That tradition now more or less destroyed, interpreters of Islam are to be found today on satellite channels and on Internet websites, hovering over the world and pronouncing on every conceivable matter, sometimes without training and often without regard to consequence. Once jurists read and argued about the Qur'an with a view to deciphering the right laws under which to live within the confines of a living tradition. Little of that edifice remains. It died after the Sykes-Picot Agreement carved up the Ottoman Empire between the British and the French in 1916—a date firmly fixed in the mind of Osama bin

Laden in his first communiqué after the September 11, 2001, attack.

There is no simple remedy to revive a body that has all but expired. The uplinked television and Internet imams will continue to stone to death the offerings of "enlightenment" that come their way. With little at stake, either because they are safely protected by immovable political powers or because they have nothing to lose, they make their declarations from a distance. From a distance, recklessness has no cost. The post-colonial segregation of religion and politics and the superimposition of the state system in the Middle East are the proximate causes of this sort of disembodied Islam, so to speak, from which the region now suffers acutely. The more distant causes are unclear. I venture that the Muslim societies of the Middle East will not find their bearings unless a juridical tradition able to work within the confines of state sovereignty arises from the ashes or until, in some distant century, Islam as a comprehensive doctrine, as a way of life, is definitively repudiated. In the interim, while the Islamic world stands between these two confounding alternatives, I cannot help but think that my students in Qatar are largely right when they tell me that constitutional monarchy is the most fitting political form for the times in which they live. Whether in the democratic age such a political form can be thought legitimate is one of the great questions we all face.

Of all the changes wrought by the democratic age to religion, both among my students in America and in Qatar, perhaps the most intriguing pertains to the proximity democratic man demands of his relationship to God. In America, as I mentioned, that demand is captured in the well-worn locution: "Jesus is my friend." For Muslims, Mohammed is understood to be the last of God's prophets, and in that sense is equivalent to Jesus—both being God's prophets. For Christians, Jesus is the God-man and one sufficient mediator, not a prophet. Given these different understandings, comparisons are difficult. Nevertheless, it is telling that on several occasions I walked past posters on the Qatar campus containing the statement "Mohammed is my friend." In Islam, Mohammed is not divine. He is, however, revered. To believe that he is a "friend" suggests a softening, a domestication, an Islam more sentimental and less austere, not unlike what has occurred to Christianity in America. Anecdotes should never stand for the whole, but what is happening among my students in the Middle East on this score is worth noting. Their religion purports to hold them fast. It would be a mistake, however, to ignore the subtle signs that the world they inhabit is being altered by the conditions of equality that soften and domesticate all relations, even those between man and God.

From Whence Comes the Idea of Equality?

When I teach the history of political thought to freshmen on the main campus, I can be certain that nearly all of them believe down to the marrow of their bones that democracy is the best political form. They do not know that the founding fathers set up a republican government, not a democratic one; or that throughout history there has been a well-founded suspicion that democracies tend to go horribly awry—indeed, if Plato is a worthy guide, they tend to devolve into tyrannies. My main campus students simply take for granted that democracy alone is worth defending; justice and equality being synonymous, what alternative is there, really? They even routinely use the phrase "the transition to democracy"—which implies that all other political forms are unstable and on their way to democracy, the final and permanent form of government. Such are our American prejudices.

Shortly after I began teaching my history of political thought course in Qatar in the fall of 2005, I discovered, as I mentioned above, that many of my students there believe that constitutional monarchy is the highest political form. When students from the main campus come to Qatar for a semester, they are surprised to learn that their love of democracy is not shared by all and are perplexed about what to do with their realization.

There is a serious question that this stark difference between my students raises, which I suspect will plague us for much of this century: From whence comes the idea of the equality of all, and on what grounds can it be defended? This is a serious question because most of man's history has been marked by the belief in inequality—indeed, in the belief that slavery is a perfectly acceptable arrangement. In human history, I remind my students, equality is the exception, not the rule. What brought about this exception that now suffuses the minds of my American students? As Tocqueville put the matter:

> All the great writers of antiquity were a part of the aristocracy of master, or at least they saw that aristocracy established without dispute before their eyes; their minds, after expanding in several directions, were therefore found limited in that one, and it was necessary that Jesus Christ come to earth to make it understood that all members of the human species are naturally alike and equal.[7]

It was Christianity that inverted the old formula: hierarchy is the very order of things. Judaism had done this long before and so was the source of this revolution; but Christianity declared it true for all the nations. From the vantage of God, on the other hand, all are created equal.

Most of my students on the main campus have other ideas. They think that equality is self-evident; or that notions of universal rights, recognition, and human dignity can rest on purely philosophical foundations; or that the quiet voice of conscience attests to such things in every human heart. Against this sort of fancy, Nietzsche, who thought that rank ordering seems to be inscribed into nature herself, wrote that the crisis of the West for the next several centuries would amount to this: unable to fully let go of Christian *religion*, man would hold on to the trappings of Christian *morality*, but go no further. Thus, his pithy aphorism: "It is the church, and not its poison that offends us."[8] In the eighteenth and nineteenth centuries, missionaries were sent to colonial lands to convert the nations to the Christian religion; my students are embarrassed. In the twenty-first century, our cosmopolitan elites are sent out to former colonial lands to assist nations to become democratic; my students are proud. Then I tell them that Nietzsche thought that Christianity and democracy were allied, and that perhaps the desire to spread democracy abroad amounts to missionary work in a new guise. The old missionaries spread Christian religion; the new missionaries spread democracy, the political manifestation of Christian morality. Living in a public world that repudiates "the church" but not "its poison," many of my students want to defend Christian morality without what they perceive to be the dead weight of the religion that gave rise to it. They cannot have it both ways. Thus spoke Nietzsche.

Tocqueville wrote in *Democracy in America* that "next to each religion is a political opinion joined to it by affinity."[9] Nietzsche agreed. But while Nietzsche indicts Christianity and democracy because only the soul mired in resentment could possibly want them, and admonished man to be a bridge to a future beyond such resentment, Tocqueville concluded that the democratic age was now definitively upon us, and that Christianity would be needed to attenuate the maladies to which delinked man is prone. For my students, it is hard to imagine two wagers about the future that are more diametrically opposed. Tocqueville sees in Christianity an ameliorative for an illness; Nietzsche sees in Christianity the cause of the illness observed.

What, for Tocqueville, follows from this "affinity" between religions and political forms? My students on the main campus want to hear that democracy is the universal political form. Tocqueville, I remind them, worried about this mindless and reflexive need for uniformity. "Variety is disappearing from within the human species," he wrote.[10] If, indeed, religion shapes the mental habits that guide man to the political form he adopts, then what can be said about the supposed universality of democracy? First and foremost, democracy may not be universal at all; second, *if* democracy is to emerge in those regions without a Christian heritage, it can only do so by relying on the religious heritage that already resides there. In the case of the Middle East, in particular, democracy will have to emerge within the context of Islam or not at all. Religion is the deepest thing; it is sheer folly to ignore the way it shapes mental habits in the Middle East—and still in America, too. That Islam, like Christianity, declares all men to be equal in God's eyes is immensely promising; that Islam is also a religion of law whose stipulations are, by many accounts, unwaveringly true suggests that it will be unable to hold sway amidst the flux of the democratic age. The fate of democracy in the Middle East swirls around these two antipodes.

Faith and Liberty

When I finally flew out of Doha in the spring of 2008, I did not go directly home to my wetland forest on the Eastern Shore. Stopping off instead in Jerusalem to assist with a controversial but important trip that took a number of students from Georgetown's Qatar campus to the Holy Land, I stayed for a few days at the American Colony House.

Eventually purchased by a number of Christian families from Chicago who banded together in 1881 and moved to Jerusalem so that they could live in a simple manner, as the early Christians had done, the leader of the group, Horatio Spafford, is best known as the author of the lyrics to the magisterial Christian hymn "It Is Well with My Soul." The circumstances surrounding the composition of the hymn give pause. In 1873 his wife, Anna, and their four young daughters boarded the SS *Ville du Havre*, bound for England. The ship never arrived. Accidentally rammed by the *Loch Earn* in the North Atlantic, the vessel sank beneath the waves in twelve minutes, in which time 226 souls perished. Anna was among the 87 survivors; her four daughters—Annie, Tanetta, Maggie, and Bessie—were not. Once ashore in England, the telegram she sent her husband read: "Saved alone." Horatio left immediately. On the journey across the Atlantic, he composed the now-famous lyrics—by some accounts as his ship plowed through the dark seas off Newfoundland where his daughters had perished.

To write "It Is Well with My Soul," shortly after the death of four young daughters—in addition to the death, earlier, of a young son from scarlet fever in 1870 and the loss of much of his wealth in the Great Chicago Fire of 1871—required an uncommon faith. The wager of such faith is that the course of man's life is in God's hands; and that, irrespective of how dire his circumstances may be, the reconciliation he seeks must emerge from and through his relationship with God and with his neighbor. Herein lays the burden of man's liberty. The hymn's lyrics point to such an understanding.

The more I think about the future prospects for liberty in America, the more I doubt that it can be maintained without an understanding that the final evaluation of our lives must be made with a view to and from Eternity rather than in light of "the short space of sixty years,"[11] as Tocqueville called man's allotted time on earth. If, in some distant future that has already been imagined, life amounts to a gluttonous feast, a frantic attempt to stave off death, an enterprise to harness both man and nature so that we may be spared from failure but kept from too much success (lest pride overcome us or envy overcome others before we pass into oblivion), then I suspect that liberty has no place. The back and forth of party politics may win for liberty small victories; but I do not think the America polity will steer a corrective course unless and until a preponderance of its citizens, in their private and in their ecclesial lives, turn and affix their gaze elsewhere. How this might occur, I cannot say. Certainly no calculated plan can bring it about. Nor am I oblivious to the immense suffering that man's darkened heart can provoke in the name of such a turn—especially when it becomes a political cause. Nevertheless, I cannot escape the conclusion that liberty for democratic man, finally, can only fully be defended within a framework in which life is a trial, a pilgrimage, an ordeal through which we are tested by adversity, exposed to the moral burdens with which such adversity encumbers us, and held responsible for the actions we perform. I, for one, wish it were otherwise; but I do not think it is.

If life is not such a trial, if between our first cry and last breath the thoughts that enthrall us involve a meal and the comforts of the hearth, keeping death at bay, and eliminating risk and its consequences, surely an efficient national government with the administrative reach to penetrate into the daily details of our lives will best serve that purpose. Godlike, it will promise to give us our daily bread, protect us from harm, soothe all wounds, and assure us that all are equal in its earthly kingdom. This was the future Tocqueville feared would befall us.

If life is not a trial, then delinked democratic man will gladly give up his liberty, provided that the state protects him *from* adversity. If life is a trial, then he must live with the agonizing understanding that God will protect him *in* adversity and that his liberty cannot be alienated.

The problem of the death *of* man invites government to take one form; the problem of the death *in* man, which only the exercise of his liberty can ameliorate, demands that it take another.

Without this latter understanding, I doubt that the federal arrangements praised throughout *Democracy in America*, which devolve political authority as no regime in history ever has, can be justified. "If [man] has no faith, he must serve, and if he is free, he must believe."[12] Thus prophesied Tocqueville.

Man, it seems, will always worship. If this is true; if, as Tocqueville seemed to believe, man *cannot help* but worship, then, humbly, and with awe and reverence, his gaze will be drawn toward God, and thence, with abiding concern, toward his neighbor; or, entranced by a lesser light, he will look proudly, with awe and in reverence, to and at the distant paternal state, to the one visible power that remains in the democratic age, and disregard his neighbor entirely. Here, too, I wish it were otherwise. I am haunted, however, by the prospect that it is not.

At long last, as I drove along the final stretch of road to my home on the Eastern Shore, I passed the Antioch Methodist Church. Gazing off into its graveyard, I remembered my many silent walks under its canopy of oak and maple in the winter and spring of 2005, and the poignant words etched on the gravestone that always drew me near. Without the insight those words confirm, that life is a trial here below, I suspect liberty in America cannot long be saved.

The pains of death are past.
Labor and sorrow cease,
And life's long warfare
Closed at last,
Her soul is found in peace.

Epilogue

When I arrived home, I had intended to resume my main campus duties at Georgetown, content that I had made a "second peace" with the Middle East, deeper than the one I had first achieved growing up in Ann Arbor so long ago. In June 2008, however, not more than a month after I returned from Doha, I was asked to fly out to visit the American University of Iraq, Sulaimani, in the Kurdish region of northern Iraq. Founded in 2006, amidst the postwar chaos, its board and then-current provost aspired to build an American-style university that would someday become one of the finer educational institutions in the region.

I am sure most of my colleagues at Georgetown thought I had completely lost my bearings. My family, friends, and neighbors wondered aloud why, after being away for so long, I would consider moving to Iraq for two years to help a fledgling university that seemed so unlikely to succeed. I did not have an answer that made sense to them, or even to me. The Iraq War of 2003 had so polarized America that it was impossible to think or talk clearly about the opportunity and challenge that building a university there presented. I flew to Sulaimani in June 2008, I confess, more out of curiosity about what I would find than because I wanted the position that might be offered. A lifetime ago, in 1960, I sat at the dinner table with my five-year-old twin sister in Kuwait and listened to my father tell us never to forget that the Iraqis believed themselves to be the most sophisticated people of the Middle East, that they had a noble political culture that could not be outdone or diminished. Haunted by a distant memory that was difficult to ignore, I wanted to see what remained of the greatness of Iraq after decades of an experiment with socialism that had devolved into tyranny, and war after agonizing war.

I was not prepared for what I found. On the Arabian Peninsula, there is, to be sure, a civilization of ancient record. The brutality of the climate and the scarcity of water, however, have fated its inhabitants, until recently, to living in sparse settlements, widely spaced. The discovery of oil and natural gas has irrevocably changed that. The vast wealth these have produced has purchased, among other things, air-conditioning and seawater desalinization, which has meant an exponential expansion in the scope and scale of its cities, along with agricultural projects that were previously unimaginable. Long accustomed to living in accordance with the severe limits the natural world imposed, the now-burgeoning cities of the Arabian Peninsula seem somehow disproportionate, as if certain habits of modesty remain, and the vast stretches of the ever-growing cities that modesty forbade to be filled had to be imported, willy-nilly, from other regions of the globe. Hence, the almost postmodern feel to so many of the cities there. This gives the casual visitor the sense that the peoples of the Arabian Peninsula are inventing a new civilization, which sometimes coalesces around, and sometimes overpowers, an older civilization that modesty prevents from expanding and belief prevents from rejecting.

In large parts of what is now called Iraq, the climate was no less brutal, especially during the summer months; but the long-flowing Tigris and Euphrates Rivers made possible trade settlements that in the course of thousands of years grew into an interconnected network of towns, overshadowed and ultimately coordinated by the great city of Baghdad. The twentieth century saw movements to modernize Mesopotamian civilization, to glorify it, to retrieve it, and finally, more recently, to preserve it. Through the various upheavals, its citizens have endured deprivation and cruelty that most Americans can scarcely imagine, the result of which is an exhaustion and, yes, servility of mind that lead many, but not all, to doubt their own powers. They live in anticipation of the insurmountable problems that tomorrow will bring and scarcely think about a distant future they can in any way command.

Pride, however, has not been completely vanquished. Octogenarians with whom I met spoke wistfully of another Iraq, a cultured and sophisticated Iraq that flourished before Saddam Hussein destroyed so many of the powerful families that made it possible. He did not, however, completely succeed. The visage of Iraq today is, consequently, a cruel contradiction, as are many, but certainly not all, of the nations that have experimented with socialism, involving a vast body of anonymous citizens who receive government stipends for work that is only nominally productive; and a remnant of the old aristocratic class, interconnected with and hovering above the apparatus of the state, whose dreams for the future of Iraq cannot be disentangled from the aspirations they have to immortalize their family name. All the equality, servility, and resentment of a socialism that devolved into tyranny—conjoined with the immense pride of name that only the aristocracy that socialism was designed to crush can produce. What can give rise to this contradiction except a civilization established and still guided by forces that the desire for equality in the democratic age can modify but never wholly eliminate? On the Arabian Peninsula, the disastrous experiment that began with socialism and ended in tyranny, from which Iraq will long carry searing wounds, never occurred. How could they when Islam plays the central role that it does? As I have suggested earlier, there is ample evidence that the de-linkage of the democratic age, which tempted Iraq and other nations of the Middle East into socialism in the first place, is now playing out on the Arabian Peninsula as well.

The failed Iraqi experiment with socialism has left most of its institutions in shambles—not least among them its universities. Quaint as it may sound, a university is an institution that must be oriented by the love of truth. Ignore or deny it, and all is lost—or soon will be. Truth, however, is both valuable in itself and also useful. A university, consequently, is caught up in a contradiction it can never resolve in principle, but must always balance in practice: it must distance itself from the society that underwrites it and also be of service to that society. The challenge of building the American University of Iraq, Sulaimani, therefore, involved being attentive to the grander mission that every university has in common: being cognizant of the opinions that community leaders, parents, and students had about what a university is supposed to do for them; and being imaginative enough to anticipate what a university would need to provide if it was to be of service to an Iraq that had been released from the terrible cruelty of Saddam Hussein— the monstrous leader who Iraqis would, in private, tell me they could not by themselves have deposed. His sons, heirs to their father's legacy, would have been more monstrous still.

From within the modest compound walls of the American University of Iraq, Sulaimani, it was difficult to say if this secret thankfulness would have been more public had life in Iraq after the fall of Baghdad on April 9, 2003, not spiraled down toward the abyss. The great American mythos, inscribed into the hearts and minds of its citizens since the Revolutionary War, is that when a tyrant is deposed, freedom springs forth spontaneously. Less generously, this is not a mythos but rather a syndrome—the King George III syndrome: remove the oppressor and then beneficent leaders, concerned with the liberty and prosperity of their people, will emerge and guide their countries toward democracy. It seldom happens that way—whether in Iraq, Libya, Egypt, or Syria. Neither the Democratic nor the Republican Party has learned this lesson well. No doubt tyrannical leaders harm their countries; but the agonizing truth is that the alternative can sometimes be worse. Such is the morally ambiguous world in which we live.

What, then, is to be made of the evident tension between

building an American-style university *in* Iraq oriented by the love of truth and the near-disintegration *of* Iraq wrought by an American foreign policy oriented by mythos? Not a day passed when this tension was not evident at the American University of Iraq, Sulaimani. In our discussions about what was to be expected from our Iraqi students, in our dealings with the board of directors there in the Kurdish region, and above all in the tremendous acrimony and deep misunderstandings that daily appeared in the relations between the ex-pats who had come to Iraq to help reconstruct a world but could not agree how, the nascent campus one day presented a picture of soaring optimism and the next day of brooding despair and simmering rage, of the clarity of mind that the love of truth promises and the spinning machinations the mind undergoes when it has grievously misjudged the world.

It is difficult for most Americans to understand the ideas about politics that came naturally into the minds of so many Iraqis during the Saddam Hussein era, and which still secretly guided the thinking of many of our students at the American University of Iraq, Sulaimani. The problem, I heard them say, is that "our politicians are not decisive." I soon discovered that the frame of reference for this peculiar phrase was Saddam Hussein, who was "decisive" because nobody dared oppose him. Saddam Hussein is gone, but the general disposition remains to think in terms of a single authoritative power, rather than of real federalism or of the long and public deliberations among citizens that democratic governance requires. The political alternatives in such a world seem self-evident: either a single man who rules over all—or chaos, anarchy, and disorder. It will take a very long time for this habit of thought to be dispelled and replaced. Perhaps it will not be replaced at all. Thinking enthralled by these two alternatives will find the idea of democratic governance quite foreign.

To be sure, there were students who wished to think of governance in other terms than the either/or of a "decisive" ruler or of wretched chaos. They were, however, more the exception than the rule. They adjudged that the minds of their compatriots had been afflicted and opposed such habits of thought, even though they did not yet possess an antidote against them. Hence, the baffling admixture of earnestness about "democracy" that was at the same time without any working knowledge of what "democracy" might actually entail—something seen not only in Iraq but also among young men and women throughout the Middle East. Only long experience with democratic governance can give them the working knowledge they need, but it is just this which is lacking. They love but do not yet have an object of love before them; and so their imagination renders a depiction of their lover that is a projection of their own deepest longings. Democratic governance requires a surer foundation than this. It must, as Tocqueville wrote, be "accomplished daily before [man's] eyes and so to speak in his hands."[1] It is the stuff of prose, not of poetry.

In America, I wonder if a strange mirror image of this problem does not afflict us today: the habit of democratic governance has become so internalized, so taken for granted, that we cannot but project it outward onto the world and see in it a self-evident and, therefore, universal remedy for all afflictions—or rather, see in it not just something medicinal, but, in fact, something salvific. Hence, the remarkably easy manner in which the conclusion is reached in America that a tranquil world order is actually achievable, and that the way forward involves the creation of a federation of democratically governed states, less likely to fight because market commerce and political representation are natural allies, united by their opposition to war. By the time I flew home from Doha in May 2008, my easy American confidence that democratic government is the true and universal *political* form had already fallen by the wayside. Tocqueville's claim that the age of democracy is upon us, it is always worth remembering, is *not* a claim that the political apparatus of democracy is inevitable everywhere. What he thought inevitable was the delinked *social* condition that I have chronicled throughout *Tocqueville in Arabia*.

It is democratic governance abroad, however, that has captivated the imagination of American foreign policy makers, and it is to that longing that my remaining comments here are addressed. Sitting in my office in northern Iraq for two years in meeting after endless meeting, I was continually brought back to the raw fact that American foreign policy had altered the course of a nation. Every decision we made at the American University of Iraq, Sulaimani, was calibrated to that indeterminate future some welcomed and others feared. I departed in August 2010 convinced that Iraq would indeed stumble into the future intact and, perhaps, even be a great nation again—but that the ebullient certainty that brought American troops to the region must never be allowed to guide foreign policy again.

How, then, should America comport itself in the Middle East today? The question cannot be answered without bringing to bear broader considerations, which often work at cross-purposes to one another.

First, there is the matter of policing the global commons. In chapter 1, I recounted the surge of national pride I felt while we sang "The Star-Spangled Banner" at Georgetown's first convocation in Doha in the fall of 2005. The age of nations, I noted, has not passed. Nor will it. Global commerce, however, requires that trade routes be protected and a modicum of peace be enforced from above. Certainly since the Second World War, America has performed that role—so effectively, in fact, that it is possible, today, to speak of "international law" without immediate embarrassment. The United Nations may declare it, but it is America that assures the enforcement of international law, or at least those portions of it that comport with national interest. The cost of policing the global commons is one of the reasons for the massive American military budget, which dwarfs that of any other nation by far.

Second, since the 1960s, Americans have been of a divided mind over two immensely costly enterprises: on the one hand, domestic reparations that purport to address lingering inequalities; and, on the other hand, foreign wars that seem so necessary if liberty is to be safeguarded. In *Democracy in America*, Tocqueville noted that Americans desire both equality and liberty, and marveled at how they were able to achieve both through the arrangements of federalism that placed a limit on national government. Since the 1960s, however, Americans have been unable to agree on the balance between these two enterprises, and so unchecked spending on those enterprises has first placated and then enlarged the constituencies of each. Now, four decades later, that arrangement has metastasized, and powerful stakeholders have taken hold of the Democratic and Republican parties and of the national government itself. Once equality and liberty were thought to be possible only through limited national government; now *domestic* equality and *foreign* liberty seem possible only through an immensely expensive national government. The cost of this four-decade rapprochement has been unsustainable for some time, and in the last decade most obviously so. Because interest rates have been held artificially low by monetary policy at the Federal Reserve, however, we should not be surprised that neither political party has found the fortitude to address the problem. Why should they when money is almost free, and the illusion continues that we live in a world without debt and payment?

While there is a very real need, then, for America to remain the policing power for the global commons in order that global commerce may proceed apace, the level of funding actually necessary for that task is obscured by a metastasized political struggle in America that shows no signs of being resolved. On the one side of this debate on military spending are those who would mix together policing power and the promotion of liberty abroad; on the other side are those who, disgusted by the cavalier use of American military power to promote liberty, would withdraw from the world and abdicate even the policing of the global commons.

Third, while it is true that commerce can be a centripetal

force that binds nations together, there are also centrifugal forces at work, some of which are the legacy of nineteenth- and twentieth-century colonialism. These, I fear, will be the source of much of the warfare in the twenty-first century, as I suggested near the end of chapter 1. Americans have, it is true, recently experimented with identity politics. Yet it is also true that America has been the only large-scale and successful immigrant nation in history because, as Tocqueville wrote, the Americans "wanted to make *an idea* triumph."[2] That idea may have emerged from the Anglo-Americans who first arrived on New England's shores, and they at times made efforts to limit its benefits only to themselves; yet the idea had an iron logic all its own and demanded that its reach be extended beyond the people who first nourished it. With the exception of the great wound of slavery from which America has yet to fully recover, in due course all of the peoples who have traveled or been brought to America's shore have lost sight of the inheritance of their identity, and largely recalibrated their vision to accord with this remarkable American *idea* of liberty. I need only recall my father's life and history to be able to grasp what is lost and what is gained as each generation succeeds the next. It is a tale almost every American can tell.

From the grand vantage point of the history of nations, this is a staggering achievement—for in much of the rest of the world, nations are defined not by an *idea*, but by the kinds of people who live there. In much of the rest of the world, domestic politics *is* "identity" politics.

This is what makes the many post-colonial nations of the world so precarious. Cobbled together by colonial powers centuries ago, most have neither the commitment to the idea of liberty that would, in principle, make them blind to the different sorts of groups encompassed within their territory, nor the relative homogeneity that many nations can still claim as their own. Condemned to this nether position that is unlikely to become either one or the other, a fierce admixture of re-enchantment or revolutionary fervor will likely rip these nations apart into "identity group" fragments or force them together by the capricious will of one man.

In the twentieth century, Europe was nearly destroyed by movements of re-enchantment or revolution. Anglo-American liberalism withstood them and prevailed. The challenge of the twenty-first century, I fear, will involve new iterations of those movements in the former colonial lands—for the reason I have explored throughout *Tocqueville in Arabia*, namely, peoples emerging from the aristocratic age are apt to respond to the delinked condition of the democratic age in dreamy ways.

It would be folly to pretend that the agonizing course of history can be fully understood or, even if understood, shortened. There do seem to be two lessons immediately in front of us, however, even if the distant horizon cannot be seen. The first is for those nations still emerging from the aristocratic age; the second is for America, which never really had an aristocratic past.

For those nations emerging from the aristocratic past, the lesson is simple to formulate and extraordinarily difficult to implement: the delinked democratic age is upon us, and it will not be possible to return to the perceived organic union of some bygone age by re-enchanting the world, or to bypass the present unease through a revolutionary upheaval that brings about a new age of communion and plenty. The lonely, delinked condition is upon us all. And now, having been delinked, we must voluntarily relink. Doing so cannot cure the wound; but it can make it less painful. That extended family networks and winner-take-all political parties are still so central in almost all of these nations suggests that Tocqueville's antidote is only barely conceivable today.

For America, the lesson is simple to formulate and not impossible to implement—at least after the illusion ends that we are not bound by the verities of payment and debt. When that distant day arrives, when government revenues actually guide expenditures, the use of military force will need to be both less and more than it is today.

Military force will need to be less because large-scale assaults to "liberate" nations do not work and quickly devolve into costly and corrupt state-building operations. That is why Special Forces operations are sometimes the better course.

Military force will need to be more because the purpose of war is not to liberate, but rather to fully eradicate a threat that the Congress, through the War Powers Act of 1973, authorizes to be *unambiguously necessary* for the vital security interests of the nation. The paradox is that this more terrible understanding of war will constrain its use and make clear to foreign enemies the full consequences of their intent to do harm. Americans should always be terrified to invoke this power; foreign enemies should be terrified to stand in its way. The extraordinarily costly intermediate stage, where the military takes upon itself the task of state-building, is only thinkable when the real constraints on spending are, for a time, obscured.

Both the lesser and greater use of military force should not be justified, however, by the Siren call to establish democratic governments elsewhere. Its defenders abroad are seldom unambiguously so, and even if they secure positions of power in their own societies through American military support, they are seldom able to steer the course they claim to want, sometimes because of the very support they have just received.

In addition, the lesser and greater use of military force should not be invoked in the name of "humanitarian intervention," or if so, only rarely. In the democratic age, suffering becomes visible in a way that it never could be in the aristocratic age; and the belief that it can be everywhere eliminated naturally comes into the mind. The causes of such suffering, however, are rarely self-evident or easily eradicable; and to thrust American military force onto the theater where suffering mysteriously appears is to become entangled in distant domestic struggles that America can scarcely understand, let alone alter. I wish this were not so, and that a good will and a conscience rightly attuned to the suffering of others could be channeled through military force to bring that suffering to an end. This chain of cause and effect seldom occurs.

If the use of military force should be both less and more than its current configuration allows—if military force, in short, is narrowly constrained but fierce within its proper purview, then a vast domain opens up for the clear and proper use of public diplomacy and hospitality through the State Department. The octogenarians from my father's generation who served so long ago will speak wistfully of another Department of State, a cultured and sophisticated Department of State that flourished before political appointments and, later, political correctness turned it into the shell of an institution it now has become. This is a problem that can only be redressed by a firm understanding that the knowledge we need cannot be secured through formal modeling, gaming simulations, or sophisticated satellite reconnaissance—but rather through the long, tiresome, and reverent study of the languages, history, and political cultures of the nations where our embassies reside, and a palpable engagement with the peoples of those nations who alone can provide what the current provocative but impotent alternatives cannot. We know each other, finally, only through face-to-face relations. This is true within nations and across them.

The failure of the Department of State to understand the importance of face-to-face relations was nowhere more evident than in Iraq, where our sometimes humiliating effort to secure even modest support for the American University of Iraq, Sulaimani, was met by the offer to send twenty-something Foreign Service officers up from Baghdad to teach our students "social media." Why provide urgently needed funds for curricular development, which would have allowed us to hire professors who could labor for years with our students so that they might someday discover that the either/or political categories of a "decisive" ruler or of wretched chaos are not exhaustive—why do that when students can be taught social media in an afternoon? Never mind that such social media seems to reinforce the delinked condition of the democratic age in the very process of supposedly linking each to all, or that the specter of that de-linkage was likely to drive our students into the dangerous imaginative territory where re-enchantment or revolution make their appeal. It is the stuff of poetry, not of prose.

Beyond the refurbishment of the State Department, the single most important American foreign policy initiative I can conceive of would involve a sustained and weighty commitment to support American-style higher education in the Middle East. The long history of American-style higher education in the region dates to the establishment of two venerable institutions: the American University of Cairo (1919) and the American University of Beirut (1866). With boards of directors in America and campuses in those cities, these two universities have educated generations of students and fostered loyalty and gratitude that tempers the generally hostile assessment of America in the region. Much of the funding for those universities is private. A nominal sum is also secured through a line item in the USAID budget for American Schools and Hospitals Abroad (ASHA), made possible by the Foreign Assistance Act of 1961. This should be expanded. Whether through this venue or another, deep and abiding support for American-style education in the Middle East may well be the single best way to secure the measure of goodwill toward America that seems to be so elusive. It need not be. Educating young men and women in the region, helping them develop an understanding of the democratic age that is now upon them—this is a gift easily given and happily received as well.

I do not doubt that the use of military force will be necessary long into the future; for the lion will not soon lie down with the lamb. I can imagine a sober future, however, after the excesses of the present moment have been purged, when such force is invoked only for the purpose of policing the global commons and for the defense of clearly defined national interests. A more substantive engagement with the other nations of the world is also needed, however. America, a middle-class commercial nation committed to the *idea* of liberty, may do a number of things badly, but higher education need not be one of them. Let that be among our offerings to the world. It is true that many nations are opposed to all or parts of American foreign policy, some violently so. The unadvertised secret, however, is that American higher education is desperately wanted nearly everywhere around the globe. With an outstretched hand, and in the measure we can actually afford, let us do our part to help. Two extraordinary years in Iraq at the American University of Iraq, Sulaimani, made clear not only what we should not do, but also what we can truly do well.

A final word about Doha, to which I was able to return again, in May 2012, for the first time since departing four years earlier. The development of the city, needless to say, continues at breakneck speed. It was, however, the ambience that I most noticed—the developing "ease of social relations," as Tocqueville would call them. In public, the mood seemed gentler, more relaxed, as if some lingering question that had hung in the air for years, unanswered, had been resolved and now need no longer be a burden. The swirling current of the democratic age had now been fully entered into, and the issue was no longer whether, but how, it was to be negotiated. I thought of Tocqueville's *Democracy in America*, marveled at the clarity of his vision, and shuddered at the perils that surely lie ahead. I do not doubt that there is much about the peoples of the Middle East that lies beyond my ken, for friendship and its confidences are not won in a few years. Nevertheless, I cannot help but think that we have found in Tocqueville a guide who understood the agony that would accompany the transition from the aristocratic to the democratic age, and the incomplete joys with which we would have to be satisfied if we wished to live together in this imperfect world.

Notes

CHAPTER TWO

1. Letter of January 1, 1856, cited in *Alexis de Tocqueville: Selected Letters on Politics and Society*, ed. Roger Boesche (Berkeley: University of California Press, 1985), p. 326.
2. Alexis de Tocqueville, *Democracy in America*, trans. Harvey Mansfield and Delba Wintrop (Chicago: University of Chicago Press, 2000), vol. II, part II, chap. 2, pp. 481–82.
3. Ibid., vol. II, part III, chap. 21, p. 614.
4. Ibid., vol. II, part I, chap. 8, p. 427.
5. See ibid., vol. II, part III, chap. 8, p. 561.
6. Ibid., vol. II, part III, chap. 11, p. 568.
7. Ibid., vol. II, part III, chap. 17, p. 615.
8. Karl Marx, *Manifesto of the Communist Party*, in *The Marx-Engels Reader*, ed. Robert Tucker (New York: Norton, 1978), p. 475.
9. Tocqueville, *Democracy in America*, vol. II, part I, chap. 1, p. 404.
10. Ibid., vol. II, part III, chap. 21, p. 613.
11. James Fennimore Cooper, *The American Democrat* (New York: Knopf, 1931), p. 233.
12. Tocqueville, *Democracy in America*, vol. II, part II, chap. 5, p. 491.
13. Ibid., vol. II, part I, chap. 1, p. 403.
14. Ibid., vol. II, part II, chap. 12, p. 511.
15. Plato, *Republic*, trans. G. M. A. Grube, in *Complete Works*, ed. John M. Cooper (Indianapolis: Hackett, 1997), bk. VII, 532d, p. 1148.
16. Tocqueville, *Democracy in America*, vol. II, part III, chap. 19, p. 602.
17. Ibid., vol. II, part I, chap. 20, p. 472.
18. Plato, *Republic*, bk. VI, 496d, p. 1118.
19. Tocqueville, *Democracy in America*, vol. I, part I, chap. 3, p. 28.
20. Ibid., vol. II, part III, chap. 17, p. 588.
21. Ibid., vol. II, part II, chap. 5, p. 491.
22. Ibid., vol. I, part II, chap. 6, p. 234.

23. Ibid., vol. I, part I, chap. 5, p. 83.
24. Ibid., vol. II, part II, chap. 4, p. 486.

CHAPTER THREE

1. Jean-Jacques Rousseau, *Émile*, trans. Allan Bloom (New York: Basic Books, 1979), bk. II, p. 78.
2. Marx, *Manifesto*, p. 496.
3. See Adam Smith, "Introduction," *The Wealth of Nations*, ed. Edwin Cannan (Chicago: University of Chicago Press, 1976), p. 2.
4. Tocqueville, *Democracy in America*, vol. II, part II, chap. 20, p. 530.
5. Ibid., vol. II, part II, chap. 13, p. 512.
6. Ibid., vol. I, part II, chap. 9, p. 271.
7. Ibid., vol. II, part III, chap. 19, p. 603.
8. Ibid., vol. II, part III, chap. 21, p. 609.
9. Ibid., vol. II, part III, chap. 19, p. 600.
10. Ibid., vol. II, part III, chap. 21, p. 616.
11. Ibid., vol. II, part I, chap. 8, p. 427.
12. Ibid., vol. II, part IV, chap. 8, p. 673.
13. Ibid., vol. I, part II, chap. 9, p. 279.
14. Ibid., vol. II, part II, chap. 12, pp. 573–74.
15. Plato, *Symposium*, trans. Alexander Nehamas and Paul Woodruff, in *Complete Works*, 177d–e, p. 462.
16. Aldous Huxley, *Brave New World* (New York: Harper & Row, 1946), p. xvii.
17. Thomas Malthus, *An Essay on the Principle of Population* (Cambridge: Cambridge University Press, 1992), chap 1, p. 14.

CHAPTER FOUR

1. St. Augustine, *City of God*, trans. Henry Bettenson (New York: Penguin, 1984), bk. I, chap. 8, p. 14.
2. Tocqueville, *Democracy in America*, vol. I, part II, chap. 9, p. 282.
3. Ibid., vol. I, part II, chap. 9, p. 280.
4. Ibid., vol. II, part I, chap. 5, pp. 419–20.
5. Ibid., vol. II, part III, chap. 13, p. 578.
6. Ibid., vol. II, part I, chap. 7, p. 426.
7. Ibid., vol. II, part I, chap. 3, p. 413.
8. Friedrich Nietzsche, "First Essay," in *The Genealogy of Morals*, trans. Walter Kaufmann (New York: Random House, 1967), sec. 9, p. 36.
9. Tocqueville, *Democracy in America*, vol. I, part II, chap. 9, p. 275.
10. Ibid., vol. II, part III, chap. 17, p. 588.

11. Ibid., vol. I, part II, chap. 9, p. 283.
12. Ibid., vol. II, part I, chap. 5, p. 419.

EPILOGUE

1. Tocqueville, *Democracy in America*, vol. I, part II, chap. 9, p. 291.
2. Ibid., vol. I, part II, chap. 2, p. 32 (emphasis in original).

Index

McDivitt, James, 112
Mesopotamian civilization,
    modernization of, 180
middle class, membership in,
    109
Middle East: anti-modern
    European thought, 38;
    de-linkage unknown to, 87;
    European colonization in, 156;
    experiments with socialism
    in, 87, 118; fundamentalism
    in, 170; higher education in,
    78–81; mosques becoming
    Islamic communities in, 167;
    nonexistence of delinked
    commercial man in, 37; "second
    peace" made with (upon return
    home), 179; students from
    (opinion of American business),
    100; temptation of socialism in,
    181
military force: future necessity of,
    191; public diplomacy and, 190;
    requirements of, 189
military spending, debate on, 186
money: capital flow and, 101;
    euphemism for making, 111;
    hearts of American students
    ruled by, 65; importance of
    (in democratic age), 60–63;
    as measure of business success
    or failure, 109; as universal
    currency, 61; value of, 64
monotheisms: acknowledged
    wound in, 143; great division at
    the heart of all, 163; heresies of,
    139; problem of evil in, 138
moon landing (1969), 11
Muslim Brotherhood, 4
Muslims: Arabic utterances as God-
    Words, 166; meaning of Qur'an

for, 165; perplexity over Fall of
    man doctrine, 140

Nafisi, Azar, xxv
nations: age of, 30, 185; defining
    of, 187; emergence from
    aristocratic age, 188; face-to-face
    relations with, 190; response to
    America, xiv; self-interest of, 151;
    substantive engagement with,
    192; in uncharted territory, 14
natural affection, 52–60, 131;
    American students oriented
    by, 59; in aristocratic age, 54;
    between man and woman, 18;
    cues not attended to, 131; ease of,
    61, 65 128, 129; romantic intrigue
    vs., 56
natural price, 99
New Deal, 9
New Testament, 130, 147
New World, pillaging of, 97
Nicene Creed, 144, 146
Niebuhr, Reinhold, 140, 151
Nietzsche, 32, 174
Not by Reason Alone, 14

Occupy Wall Street movement, 106
On the Incarnation (St. Athanasius),
    145
On the Origin of Species (Darwin),
    123
opportunity: equality of, 107; lack
    of, 121
original sin, xxi–xxiii
Orthodox Judaism, 157
outcome: equality of, 107, 108;
    measurable, 76, 80, 114

Persian Letters (Montesquieu),
    xxv

shaped by understandings and
misunderstandings of, xxvi
Smith, Adam, 19, 21, 89, 96, 98,
102; debate over, 73; difficulty of
teaching, 32; market commerce
advocated by, 108
social equality, 55, 61; conditions
of, 90, 93, 106, 124, 130, 136;
relations between sexes and, 130;
salutary benefits of, 65
socialism: bourgeois, 95, 123;
European vestiges of, 106; failed
Iraqi experiment with, 181;
Middle East experiments with,
87, 118
"social justice," 90
"social media," 190
social mobility, 97
social relations: ease of, 52–60,
61, 65, 128, 192; long-inherited
(abandonment of), xv
society, reproduction of, 126–34
Society of the Muslim Brothers, The
(R. Mitchell), 6
soliloquy, 64–70; collapse into, 67;
encounter with the world in the
form of, 66; as nodal point of
human experience, 69, 70
Spafford, Horatio, 175–76
stewardship: call to, 126; falling
short in, 142
suffering, meaning of, 147–51
sustenance. *See* household
(sustenance and reproduction)
sympathy, 52–60; Tocqueville's
endorsement of, 58; universal,
59; unknown, 56
Systema Naturæ (Linnaeus), 123

tax policy, 120
theodicy problem, 138

think tanks, 2
Tocqueville, Alexis de: "affinity"
between religions and political
forms, 174; concern for religious
orthodoxy by, 156; difficulty of
teaching, 32; distant prophesy of
democratic man, 93; project of
national governments described
by, 114. *See also Democracy in
America*
"too big to fail" (2008), 94
Tower of Babel construction of
man, xx
Twenty-Third Psalm, 154
tyranny, socialism devolved into
(Iraq), 181

unity: of all knowledge, 163;
brought about by God, 18;
ecumenical, 164; innocent, 33;
man's idea of, xv; as obsession,
xxvii
Universal Brotherhood of Man, xvi
universality, Christian aspiration
for, 164
universal salvation, doctrine of, 165
university, contradiction of, 182
USAID budget, 191

Vatican II, 161
Vietnam draft, 10
Ville du Havre, SS, 175

warfare, twenty-first century, 187
War Powers Act of 1973, 189
Wealth of Nations, The (Smith), 21,
89, 96, 98, 102, 108
well-being: as chief aspiration (in
democratic age), 103; concern
for (in democratic age), 154;
search for, 108